RAND McNALLY

Kids' U.S. Road Atlas

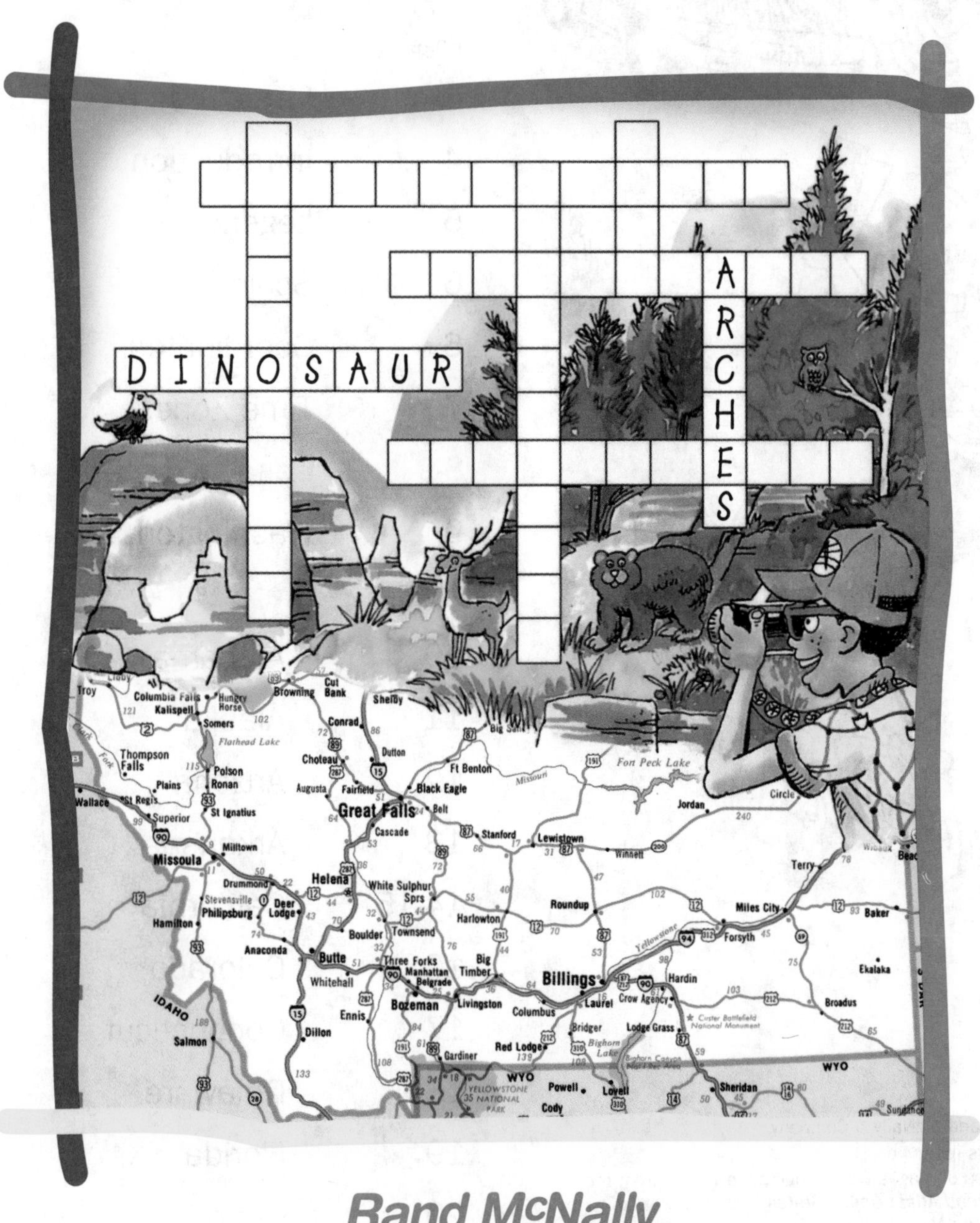

Rand McNally for Kids™

CONTENTS

INTRODUCTION

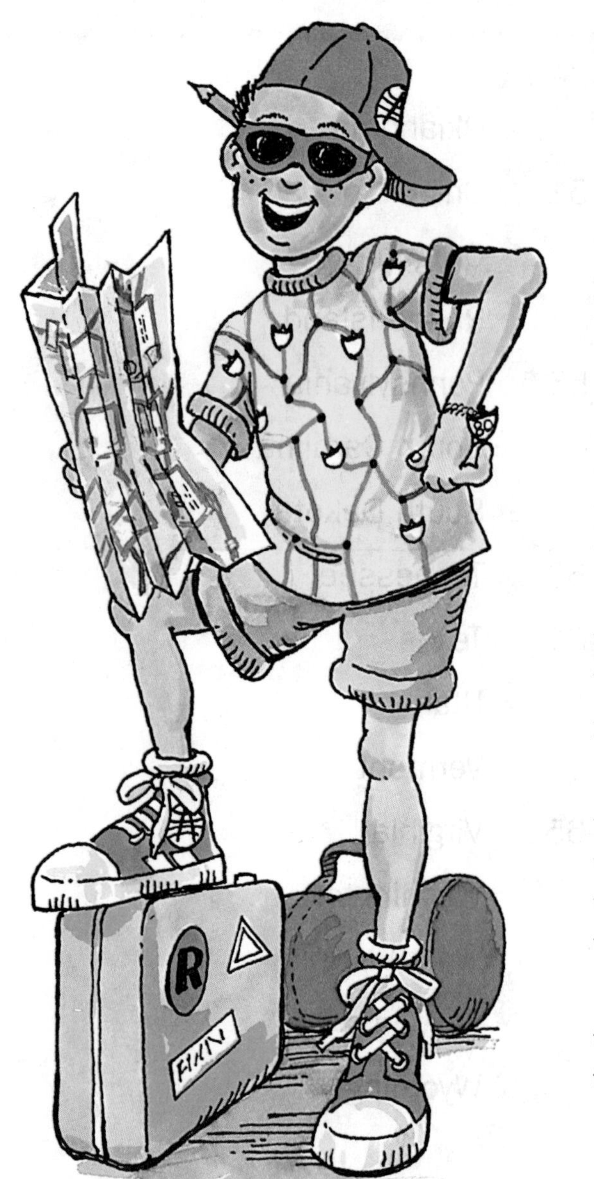

Meet Randy McNally. He's a travelin' kid just like you. And, like you, he gets bored sitting in the back seat. So, he invented the Randy McNally Kids' U.S. Road Atlas.

This atlas has real maps of all fifty states, Canada, and Mexico. You can follow along as you ride, or use the maps at home to plan a trip with your family.

Each state has its own page with a state map; a map of the whole country to show you where the state is located; pictures of the state bird, tree, and flower; and a great game or activity, often related to the state.

These travel-time games were designed to help the time fly as you ride along in the car. Some of them will sharpen your map reading skills, some of them will tell you interesting things about the states, and all of them will help to pass the time between rest stops.

The games are for kids of all ages. Many of them can be played alone, but several of them can also be played by more than one person. The only supplies you will need are a pencil, crayons, and coins or other markers.

At the beginning of the atlas is a section that will teach you how to find places on a map with the help of the index, how to tell how far it is between places, how to read the symbols on a map, and how to understand the different time zones around the world.

Randy says "Grab your book and supplies, hop in the back seat, and buckle up." You and Randy are ready to go for the best trip you've ever had. Have fun!

HOW TO USE AN ATLAS

LEGEND

The legend is a description of how the symbols and lines on the map relate to those on the earth. It is often a list of symbols and lines, each followed by a description telling what that symbol on the map means.

Roads may be of several kinds. In order to tell what kind of road you will be following, you may look in the legend to see, for example, what is a red road. The legend says that it is a principal through highway, which means that it is an important road.

Toll } Multilane Controlled Access
Free

Principal Through Highways

Other Highways

Other symbols will tell you the number of the highway, so that you can follow the number as you travel along the highway.

55 National Interstate Highways

60 U.S. Highways

49 State and Principal Highways

Trans-Canada Highway

If a city is very large, covering quite a lot of space on a map, the area of the city may be lightly colored, so that you may see how much land it covers. Large areas, such as national parks may also be colored to show how big they are. Smaller cities do not cover a large area, so they are only shown on the map by a dot. State capitals often have a special symbol, a star in a circle.

City Areas

Park Areas

City

Capital City

Some maps have special symbols to show certain features on the earth, such as an airplane to show an airport or a pine tree to show a state park. There are many such symbols, and they are different on each map, so you must look in the legend to identify any special symbols you may find on each map you are using.

Airport

State Park

Swamp

Golf Course

SCALE

A map is a kind of picture of how the earth looks, but much smaller. Maps come in all sizes, some that show the whole world, and some that show only your neighborhood. The map scale tells us how space on a map equals distance on the earth. Scale is used to measure distances between places on a map.

A typical scale will tell you that one inch on the map equals 100 miles on the earth's surface. Scale is often shown in a drawing that looks like this.

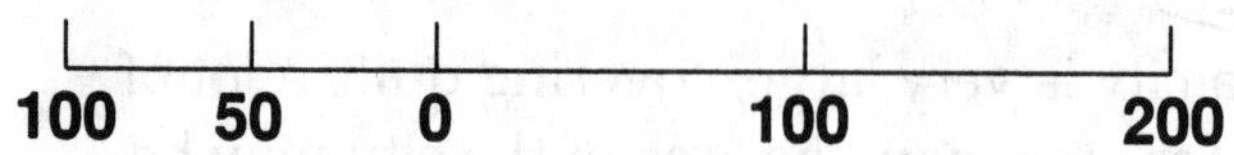

If you were planning a trip, it would be good to know how far you would be traveling. Suppose you wanted to travel from Baltimore, Maryland to Philadelphia, Pennsylvania. Take a strip of paper and lay it on the map so that its edge makes a line between the two cities. Make a mark on the paper at each city's location. Next place the strip of paper so that the mark for Baltimore matches the 0 on the scale. Now read along the line until you reach the other mark. You will see that these cities are just about 100 miles apart.

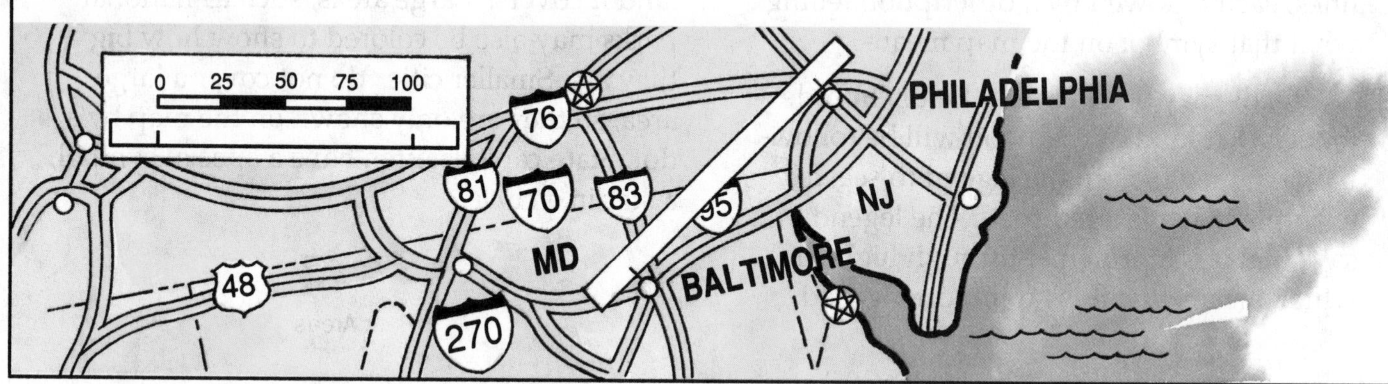

COORDINATES

A coordinate is a letter/number combination that helps you find places on a map. To locate a city, look in the index and find the coordinate for the city. If, for example, Denver has the coordinate B-5, look down the side of the Colorado map for the letter B and draw an imaginary line across the map. Then, look across the top or bottom of the map for the number 5 and draw an imaginary line down or up until it crosses the imaginary line drawn from the letter B. The city will be inside the square around this point.

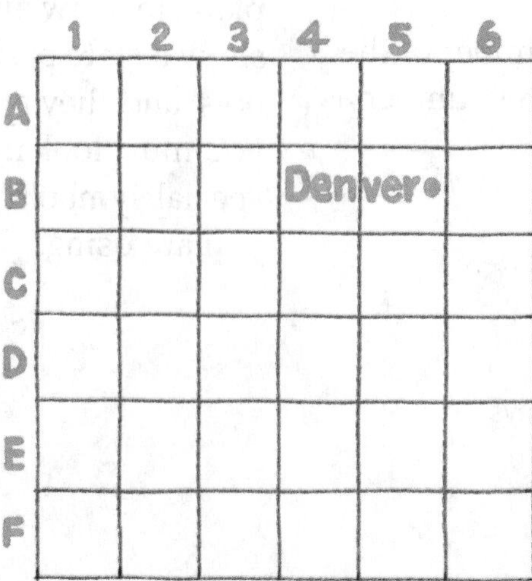

TIME ZONES

The world is divided into 24 time zones, one for each hour of the day. The lines that divide the world into equal parts from north to south are called longitude. Since they go all around the world in a circle, and a circle has 360 degrees, the world is divided into two groups of 180 degrees of longitude (totaling 360 degrees) beginning at 0 degrees. This imaginary line runs through Greenwich, England near London, and is called the Prime Meridian. From this line at 0 degrees, the longitudes are numbered both east and west until they meet at the other side of the world at 180 degrees. Time zones are not regular in shape as longitudinal sections would be, because they often follow state and national borders.

The meeting place at 180 degrees is called the International Date Line, and it runs through the Pacific Ocean east of New Zealand and west of most of Alaska. Time changes a day when you cross this line. Someone traveling west across the line adds a day and someone traveling east subtracts a day. If you leave Samoa (170 degrees west) on Tuesday and fly to Fiji on the other side of the International Date Line, when you arrive it will be Wednesday. If you return on Friday, when you reach Samoa it will be Thursday.

In the United States there are six time zones. The lower 48 states are divided, from west to east, into Pacific, Mountain, Central, and Eastern time zones. Alaska and Hawaii each has its own time zone. This means that if you were telephoning from Washington, D.C. at 10 a.m. to Honolulu, Hawaii, it would only be 5 a.m. there, and your call would probably get the person you called out of bed. A person in Alaska calling someone in Memphis at 10 p.m. would probably also awaken the party called, because it would be 1 a.m. in Memphis. If you are calling elsewhere in the world, it is very important to know what time it is at the destination of your call.

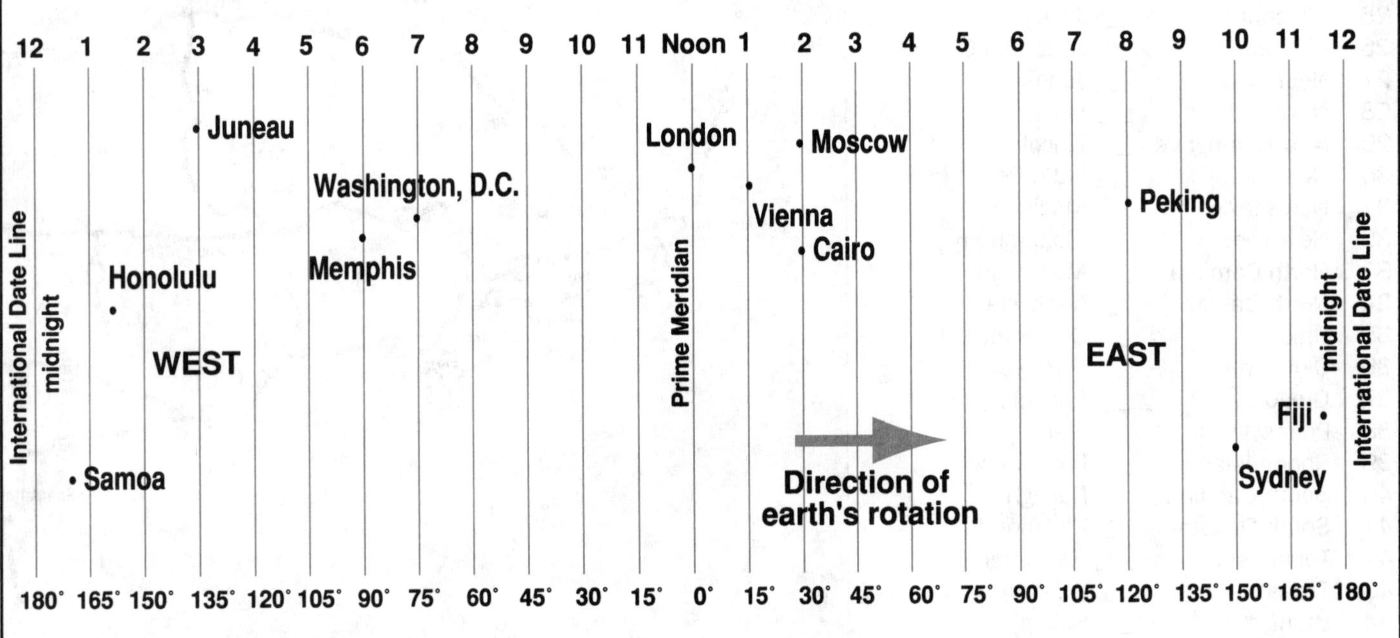

UNITED STATES MAP

Match state name with its capital!

1	Alabama	___ Albany
2	Alaska	___ Annapolis
3	Arizona	___ Atlanta
4	Arkansas	___ Augusta
5	California	___ Austin
6	Colorado	___ Baton Rouge
7	Connecticut	___ Bismarck
8	Delaware	___ Boise
9	Florida	___ Boston
10	Georgia	___ Carson City
11	Hawaii	___ Charleston
12	Idaho	___ Cheyenne
13	Illinois	___ Columbia
14	Indiana	___ Columbus
15	Iowa	___ Concord
16	Kansas	___ Denver
17	Kentucky	___ Des Moines
18	Louisiana	___ Dover
19	Maine	___ Frankfort
20	Maryland	___ Harrisburg
21	Massachusetts	___ Hartford
22	Michigan	___ Helena
23	Minnesota	___ Honolulu
24	Mississippi	___ Indianapolis
25	Missouri	___ Jackson
26	Montana	___ Jefferson City
27	Nebraska	___ Juneau
28	Nevada	___ Lansing
29	New Hampshire	___ Lincoln
30	New Jersey	___ Little Rock
31	New Mexico	___ Madison
32	New York	___ Montgomery
33	North Carolina	___ Montpelier
34	North Dakota	___ Nashville
35	Ohio	___ Oklahoma City
36	Oklahoma	___ Olympia
37	Oregon	___ Phoenix
38	Pennsylvania	___ Pierre
39	Rhode Island	___ Providence
40	South Carolina	___ Raleigh
41	South Dakota	___ Richmond
42	Tennessee	___ Sacramento
43	Texas	___ St. Paul
44	Utah	___ Salem
45	Vermont	___ Salt Lake City
46	Virginia	___ Santa Fe
47	Washington	___ Springfield
48	West Virginia	___ Tallahassee
49	Wisconsin	___ Topeka
50	Wyoming	___ Trenton

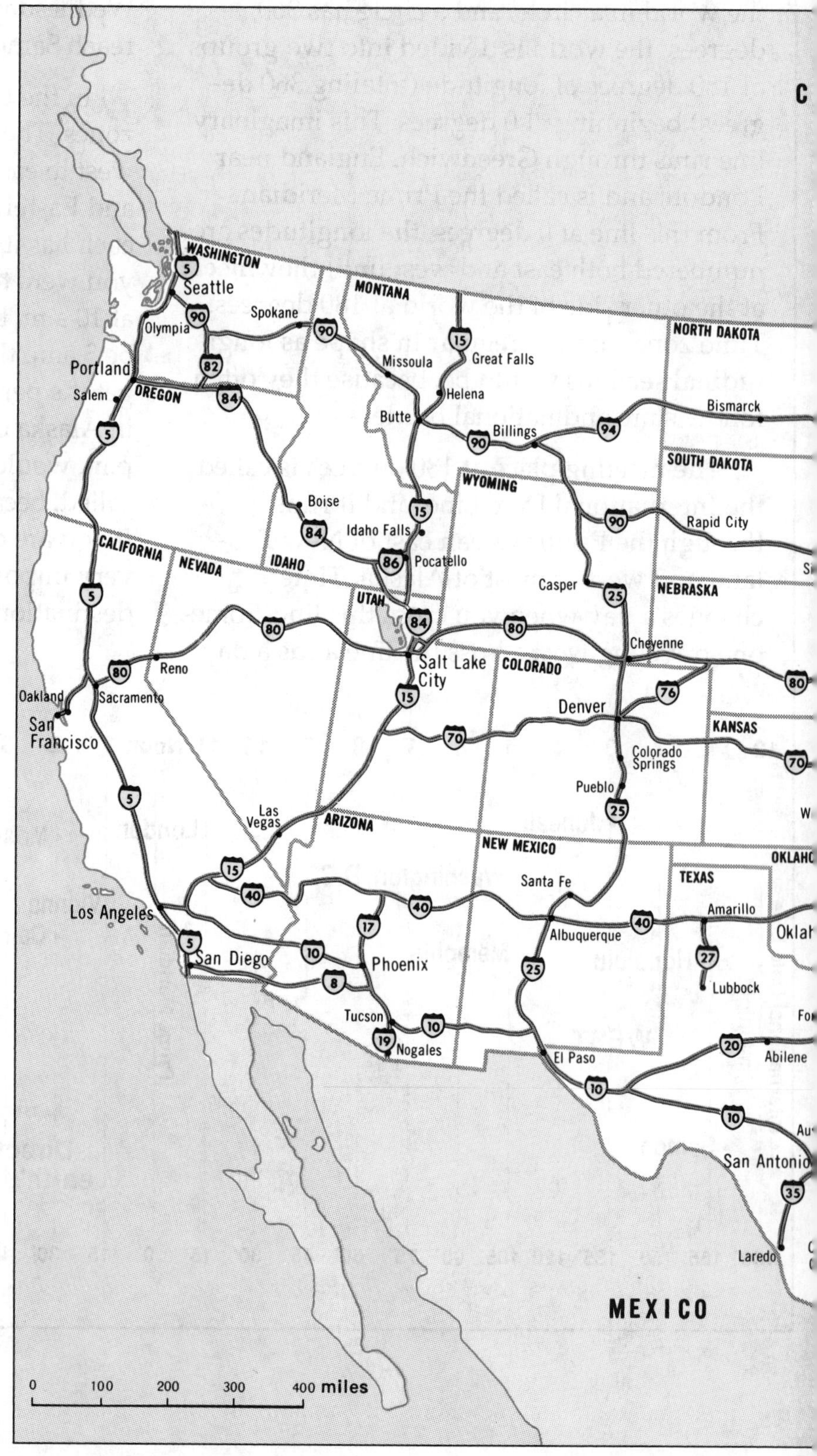

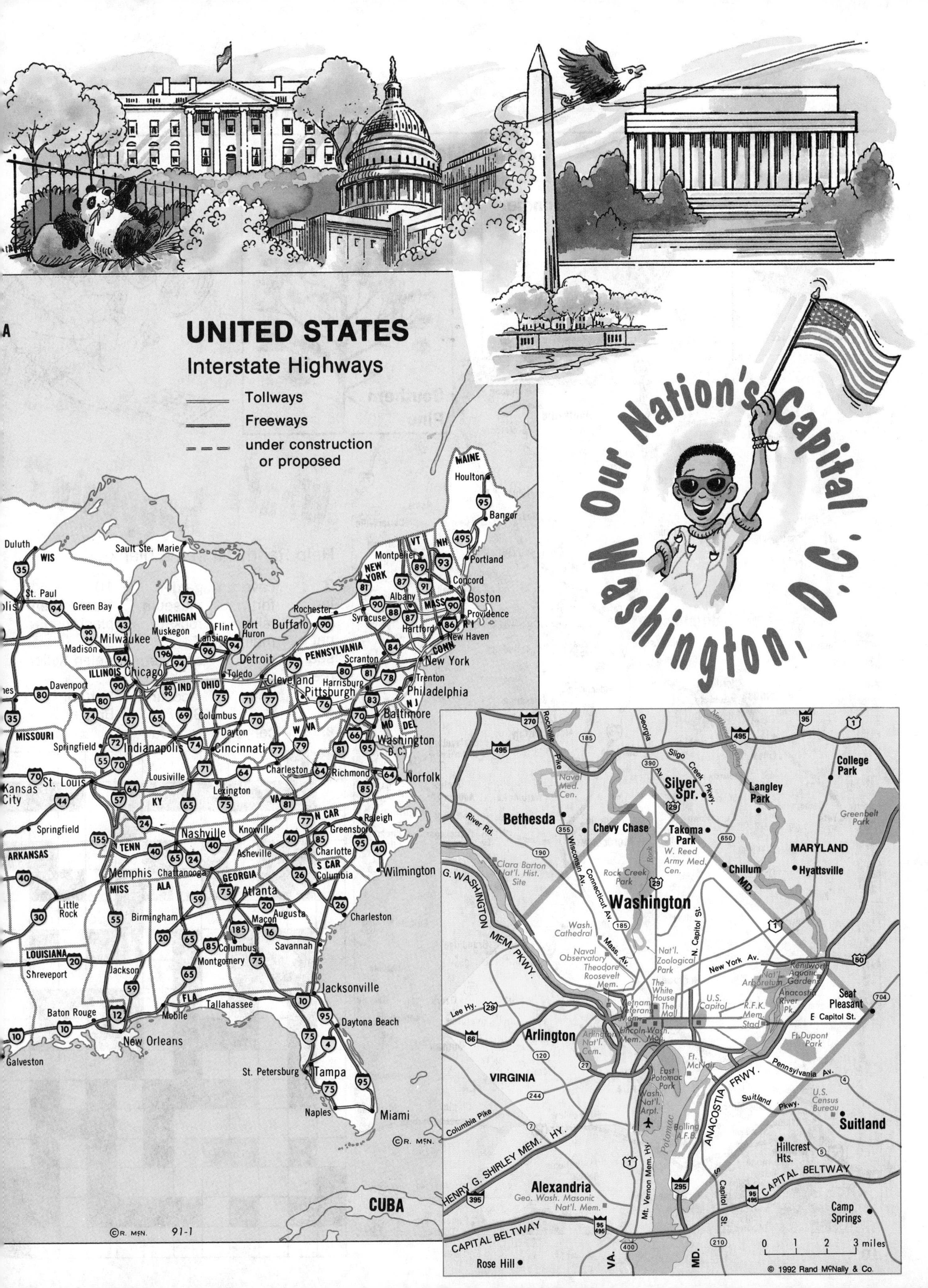

UNITED STATES
Interstate Highways
Tollways
Freeways
under construction or proposed
Our Nation's Capital
Washington, D.C.
MAINE
Houlton
Bangor
Portland
VT
NH
Montpelier
Concord
NEW YORK
Albany
Boston
MASS
Providence
R I
Hartford
New Haven
CONN
New York
Rochester
Syracuse
Buffalo
Scranton
PENNSYLVANIA
Harrisburg
Trenton
Philadelphia
N J
Pittsburgh
Cleveland
Baltimore
MD
DEL
Washington D.C.
W VA
VA
Richmond
Norfolk
Charleston
Duluth
WIS
Sault Ste. Marie
St. Paul
Green Bay
MICHIGAN
Muskegon
Flint
Port Huron
Lansing
Milwaukee
Madison
Detroit
Toledo
ILLINOIS
Chicago
IND
OHIO
Davenport
Columbus
Dayton
Cincinnati
Indianapolis
MISSOURI
Springfield
St. Louis
Kansas City
Louisville
Lexington
KY
Springfield
Nashville
TENN
Knoxville
Asheville
N CAR
Greensboro
Raleigh
Charlotte
S CAR
Columbia
Wilmington
Charleston
ARKANSAS
Memphis
Chattanooga
GEORGIA
Atlanta
Augusta
Macon
Savannah
MISS
ALA
Little Rock
Birmingham
Columbus
Montgomery
LOUISIANA
Shreveport
Jackson
Jacksonville
FLA
Tallahassee
Mobile
Baton Rouge
New Orleans
Galveston
Daytona Beach
St. Petersburg
Tampa
Naples
Miami
CUBA
©R. McN.
©R. McN. 91-1
Rockville Pike
Georgia Av.
Sligo Creek Pkwy.
College Park
Silver Spr.
Langley Park
Naval Med. Cen.
Bethesda
Chevy Chase
Takoma Park
Greenbelt Park
River Rd.
Wisconsin Av.
W. Reed Army Med. Cen.
MARYLAND
Clara Barton Nat'l. Hist. Site
Rock Creek Park
Chillum
Hyattsville
G. WASHINGTON MEM. PKWY.
Connecticut Av.
Washington
N. Capitol St.
Wash. Cathedral
Mass. Av.
Naval Observatory
Theodore Roosevelt Mem.
Nat'l. Zoological Park
New York Av.
Kenilworth Aquatic Gardens
Nat'l. Arboretum
Anacostia River Pk.
Lee Hy.
The White House
The Mall
U.S. Capitol
R.F.K. Mem. Stad.
Seat Pleasant
E Capitol St.
Vietnam Veterans Mem.
Lincoln Mem.
Wash. Mon.
Arlington
Arlington Nat'l. Cem.
Ft. McNair
Ft. Dupont Park
VIRGINIA
East Potomac Park
Pennsylvania Av.
ANACOSTIA FRWY.
Wash. Nat'l. Arpt.
Suitland Pkwy.
U.S. Census Bureau
Suitland
Columbia Pike
Potomac
Bolling A.F.B.
HENRY G. SHIRLEY MEM. HY.
Mt. Vernon Mem. Hy.
Hillcrest Hts.
CAPITAL BELTWAY
Alexandria
Geo. Wash. Masonic Nat'l. Mem.
S. Capitol St.
Camp Springs
CAPITAL BELTWAY
Rose Hill
VA.
MD.
0 1 2 3 miles
© 1992 Rand McNally & Co.

ALABAMA

Capital: Montgomery

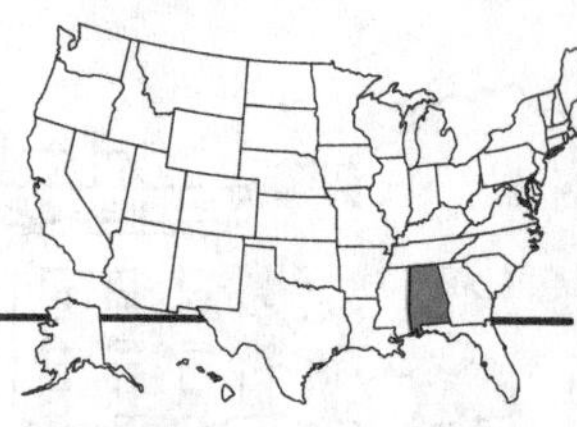

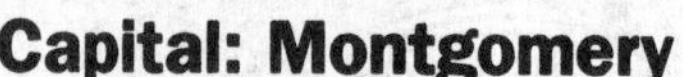

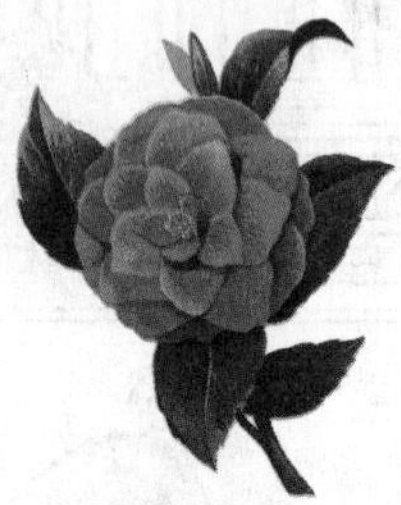

Camellia

Yellowhammer

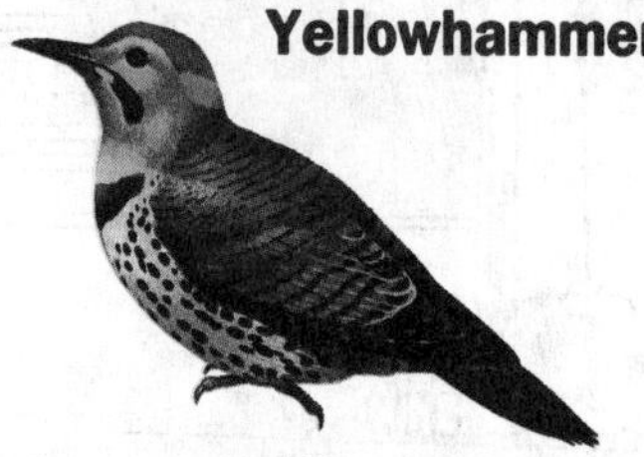

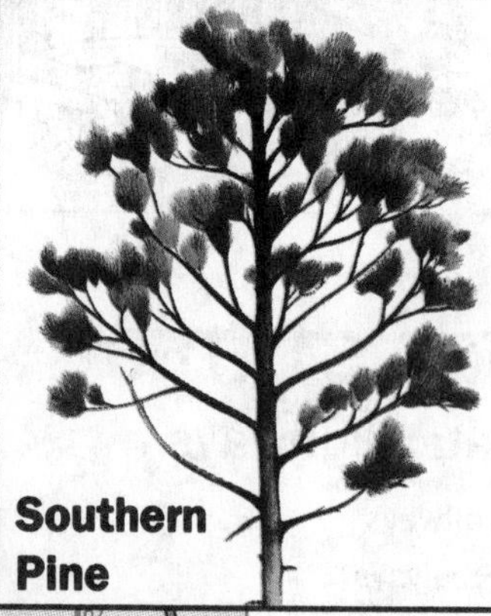

Southern Pine

What's Happenin'?

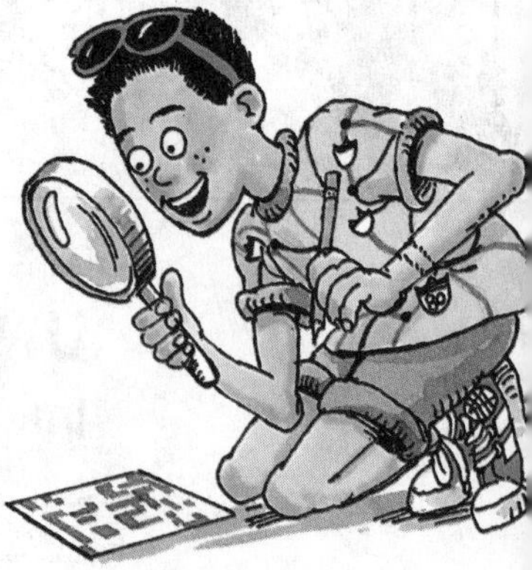

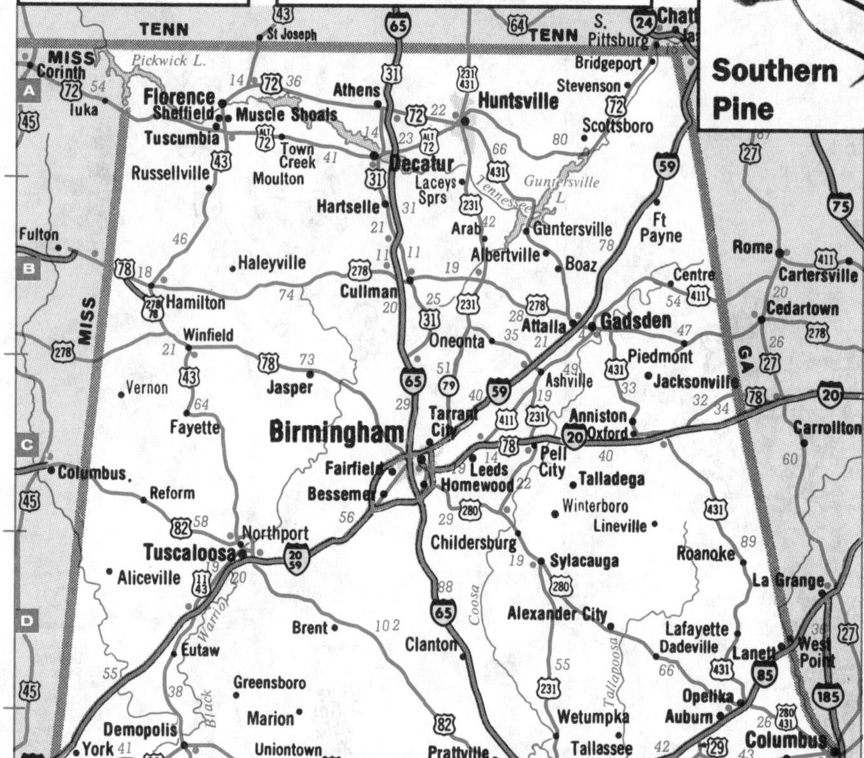

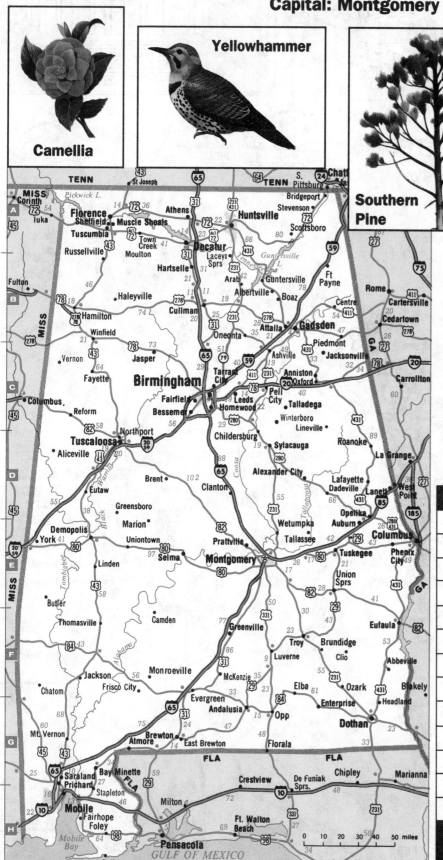

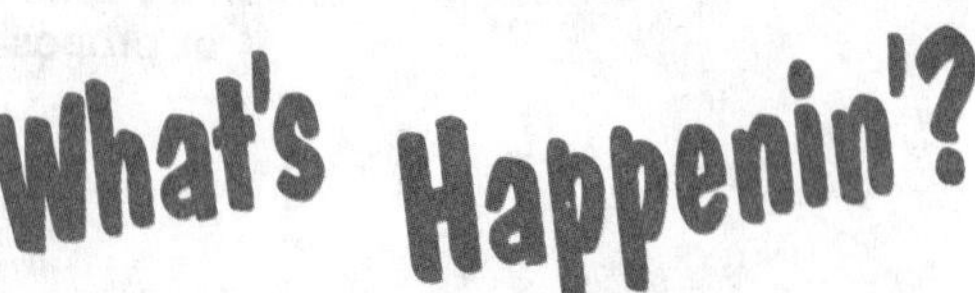

Help Randy fill in the blanks.

3	cave	garden	10
inn	fort	museum	Montgomery
ivy	lake	rocket	plantation
net	mall	7	11
sea	mill	azaleas	Helen Keller
tee	race	capitol	13
zoo	ship	racecar	Natural
4	6	9	Bridge
area	canyon	waterfall	

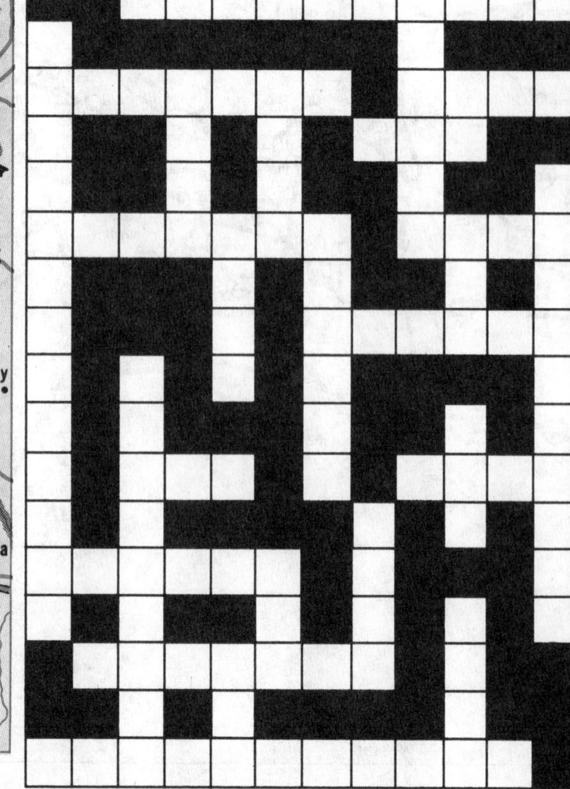

ALASKA

Capital: Juneau

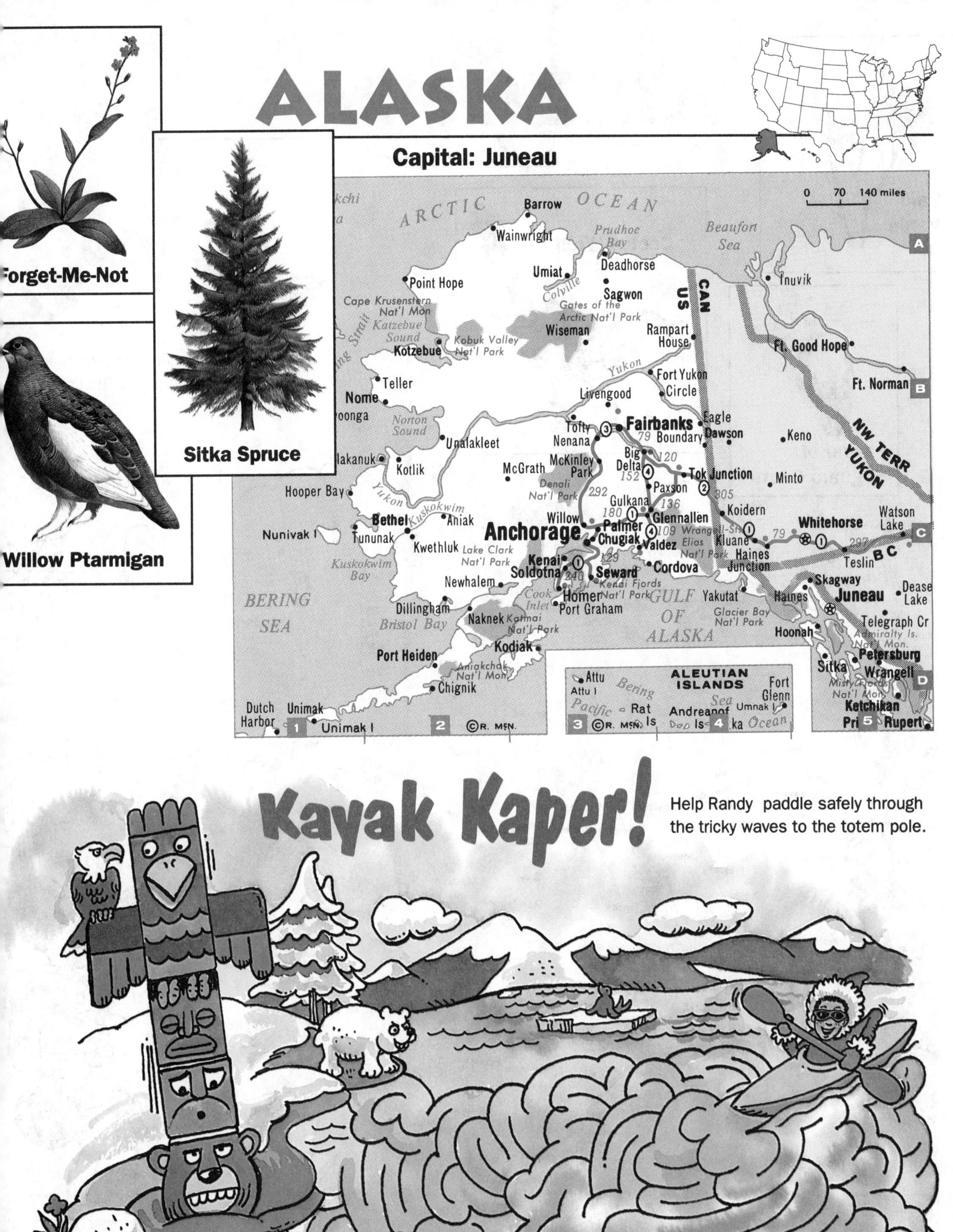

Kayak Kaper!

Help Randy paddle safely through the tricky waves to the totem pole.

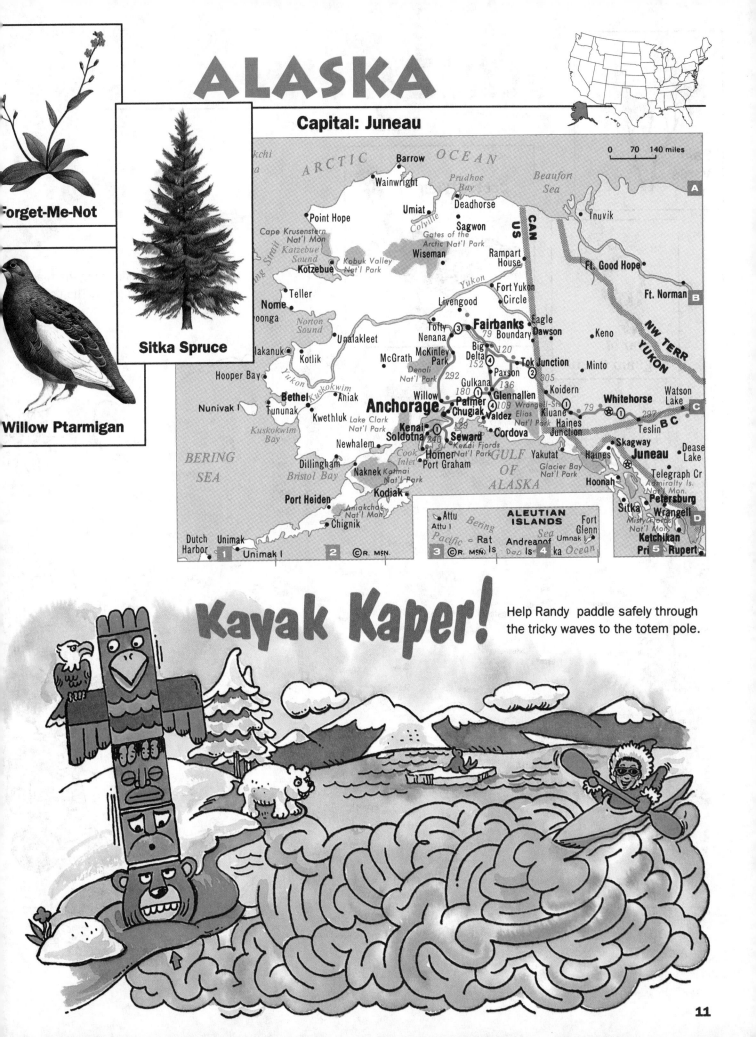

Palo Verde

ARIZONA

Capital: Phoenix

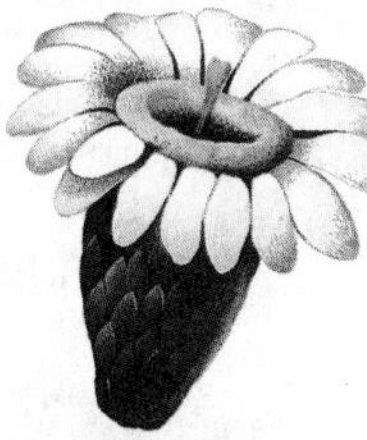

Cactus Wren

Flower of Saguaro Cactus

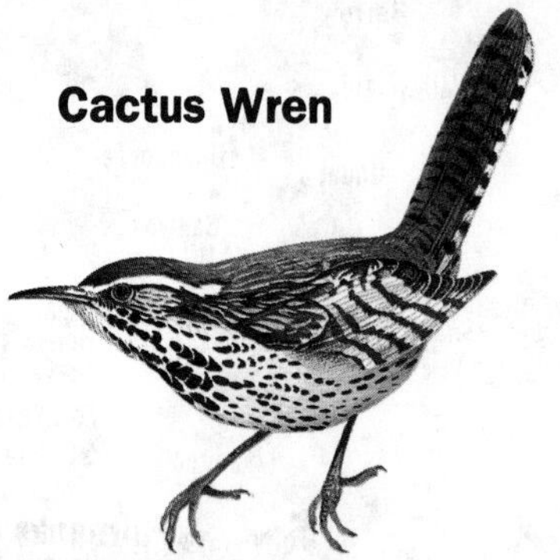

UTAH
NEV
COLO
ARIZ
N MEX
CALIF
UNITED STATES
MEXICO
SONORA
GULF OF CALIFORNIA
Cedar City
St. George
Fredonia
Page
Kayenta
Tonalea
Tuba City
Hotevilla
Keams Canyon
Chinle
Ganado
Grand Canyon
N Rim
Cameron
GRAND CANYON NAT'L PARK
LAKE MEAD NAT'L RECREATION AREA
Lake Powell
GLEN CANYON NAT'L REC AREA
CANYON DE CHELLY NAT'L MON
WUPATKI NAT'L MON
PETRIFIED FOREST NAT'L PARK
North Las Vegas
Las Vegas
Henderson
Boulder City
Peach Sprs
Kingman
Seligman
Williams
Ash Fork
Flagstaff
Winslow
Holbrook
Lupton
Bullhead City
Yucca
Needles
Lake Havasu City
Clarkdale
Cottonwood
Sedona
Camp Verde
Prescott
Snowflake
St Johns
Show Low
Springerville
Payson
Parker
Wickenburg
Wenden
Blythe
Ehrenberg
Sun City
Glendale
Avondale
Scottsdale
Mesa
Tempe
Phoenix
Chandler
Apache Jct
Miami
Globe
Superior
San Carlos
Morenci
Clifton
Hayden
Florence
Coolidge
Casa Grande
Gila Bend
Wellton
Yuma
Somerton
Tacna
Ajo
ORGAN PIPE CACTUS NAT'L MON
Eloy
Mammoth
San Manuel
Safford
Duncan
Tucson
S. Tucson
Willcox
Bowie
Benson
St David
Sells
Green Valley
Tombstone
Paradise
Nogales
Bisbee
Douglas
Agua Prieta
0 10 20 40 60 80 100 miles
91-1
©R. McN.

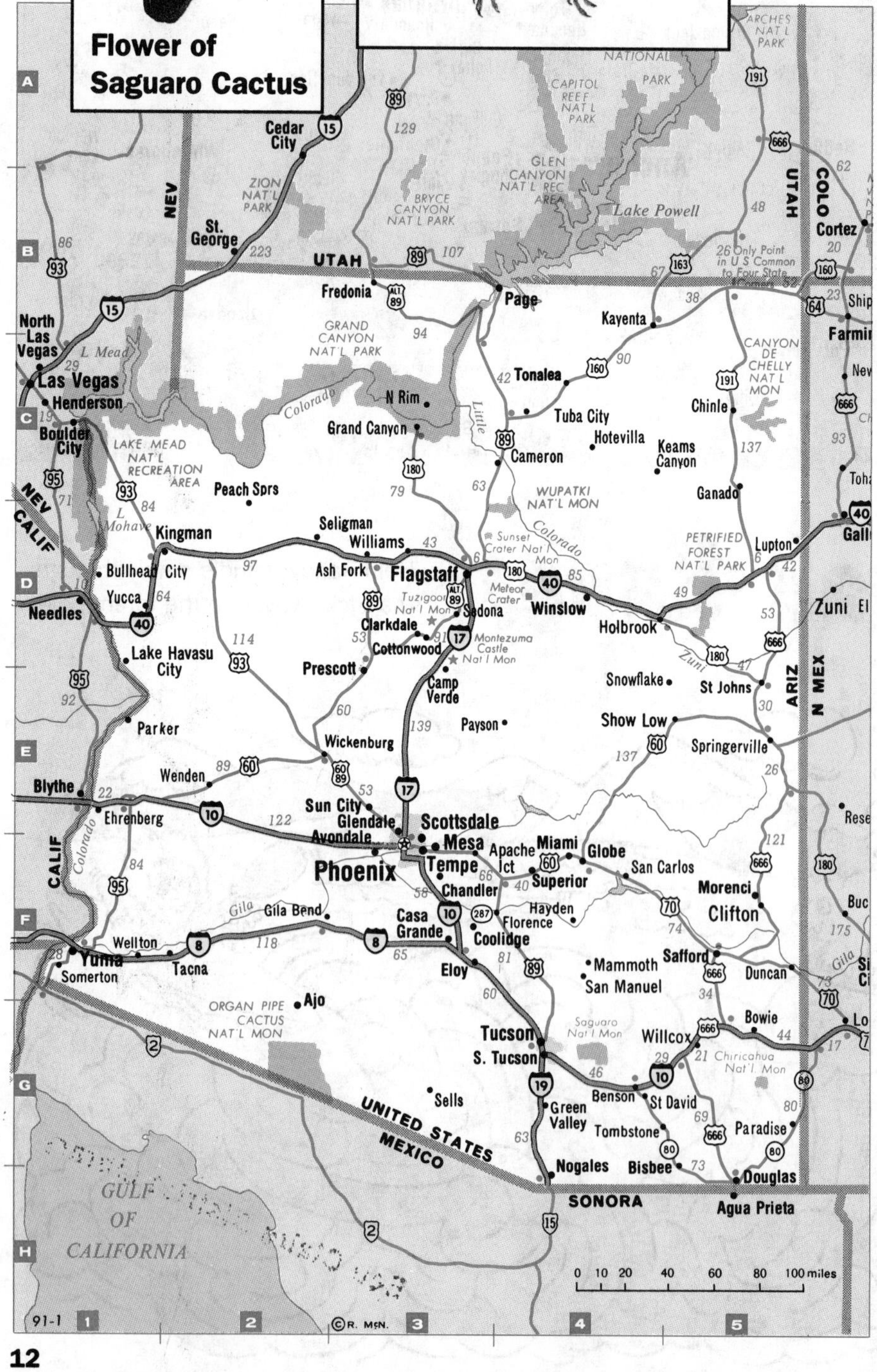

Prickly Pic!

See what Randy found along the road by following the dots in order. Then color the picture.

ARKANSAS

Capital: Little Rock

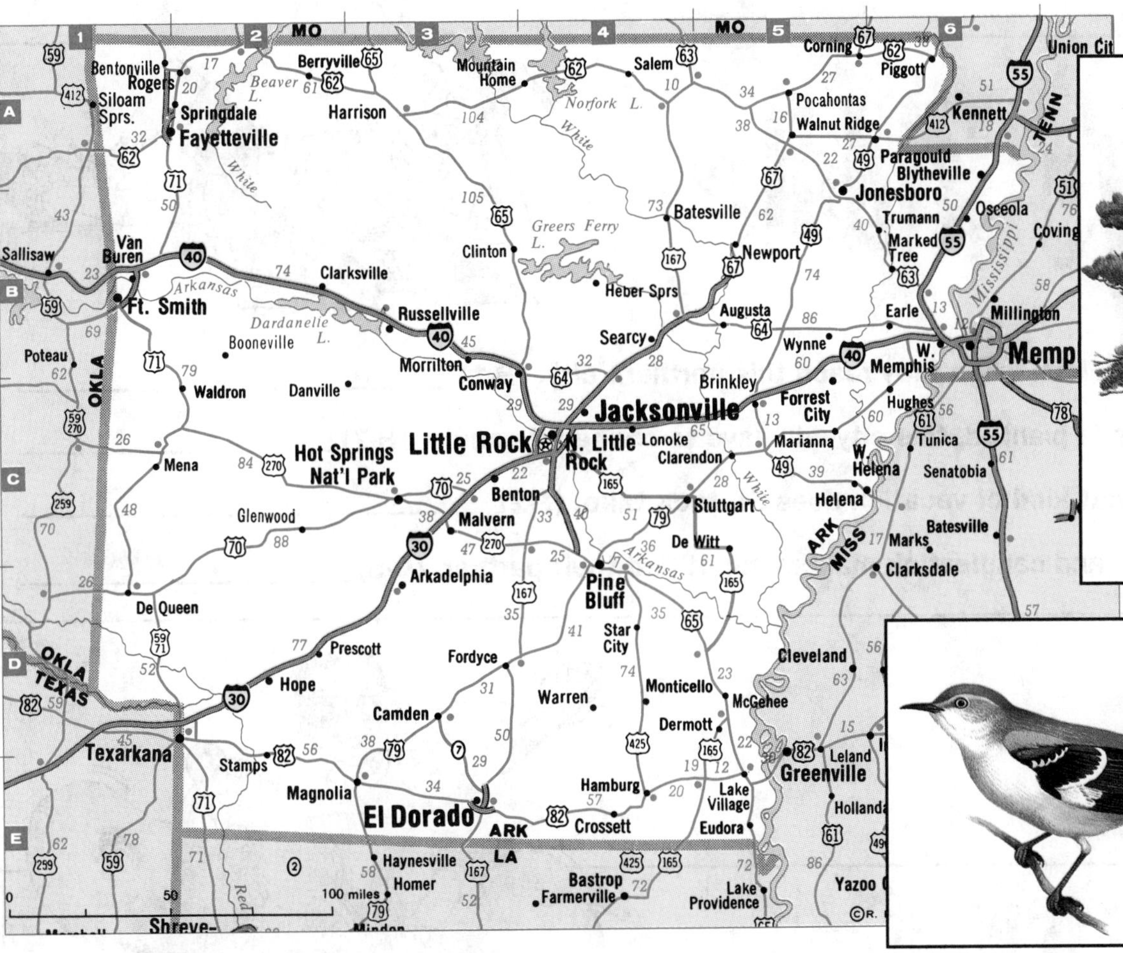

Pine

Mockingbird

Apple Blossom

Hi Neighbor!

Arkansas has seven nearby states. Help Randy spell them out. Start at the arrow and write every other letter until you have gone around the circle twice.

1. T _ _ _ _ _ _ _ _
2. L _ _ _ _ _ _ _ _
3. M _ _ _ _ _ _ _ _ _ _
4. K _ _ _ _ _ _ _
5. M _ _ _ _ _ _ _
6. O _ _ _ _ _ _ _
7. T _ _ _ _

CALIFORNIA

Capital: Sacramento

Randy's Riddles

1. **What visitors exclaim when they reach this northern city. (B-1)** ______________
2. **If one more tree is planted, this city will have to change its name. (H-7)** ______________
3. **In California, what kind of vacation does St. Nick take. (F-2)** ______________
4. **Where butchers and candlestick makers might find their partner. (G-5)** ______________

California Is Wild!

Find the home cities of these California animal parks on your map, and put them in the order you'd visit them if you were traveling north to south. Roar!

1. **San Diego Wild Animal Park (Escondido)** ______________
2. **Los Angeles Zoo** ______________
3. **Monterey Bay Aquarium** ______________
4. **Oakland Zoo** ______________
5. **The Living Desert (near Palm Springs)** ______________
6. **San Diego Zoo** ______________
7. **Sea World (San Diego)** ______________
8. **San Francisco Zoo** ______________
9. **Marine World Africa U.S.A. (Vallejo)** ______________
10. **Santa Barbara Zoo** ______________

The town name appears following the park name, if it is not part of the park name.

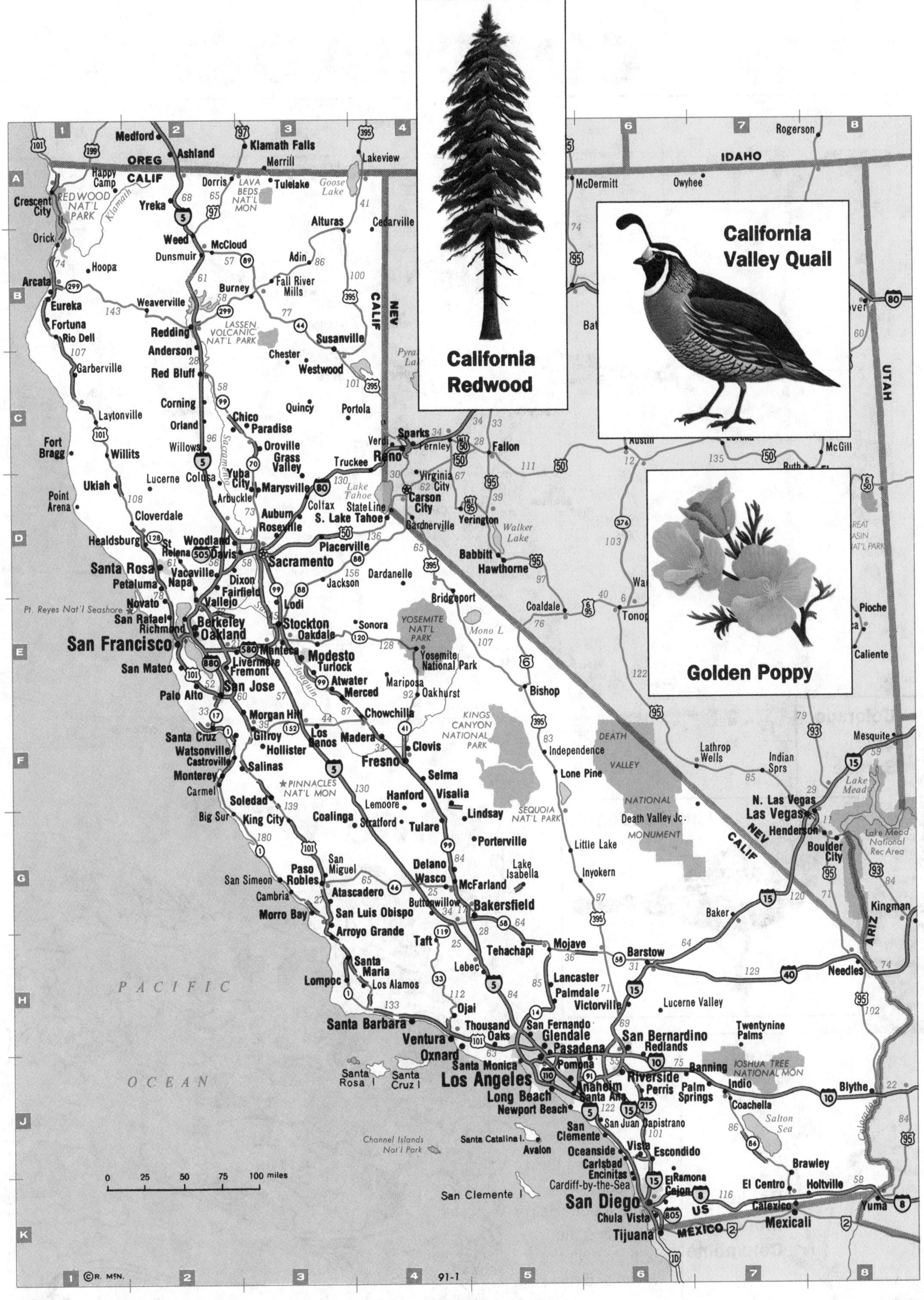
California Redwood
California Valley Quail
Golden Poppy
PACIFIC
OCEAN
OREG
CALIF
IDAHO
NEV
UTAH
ARIZ
MEXICO
US
San Francisco
Los Angeles
San Diego
Sacramento
Fresno
San Jose
Oakland
Reno
Las Vegas
©R. McN.
91-1

COLORADO

Capital: Denver

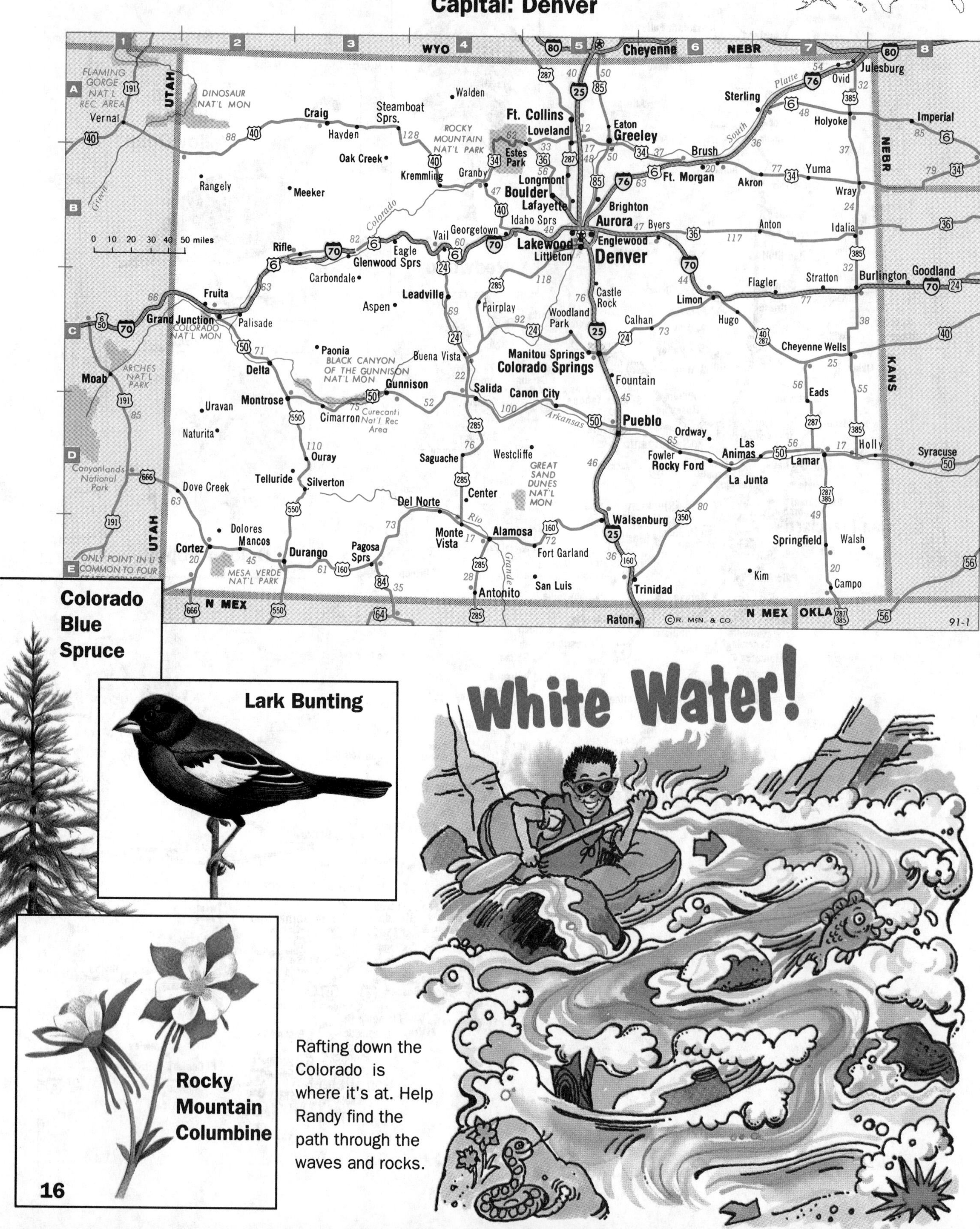

Rafting down the Colorado is where it's at. Help Randy find the path through the waves and rocks.

CONNECTICUT

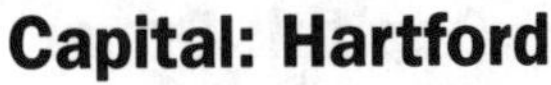

Mountain Laurel

American Robin

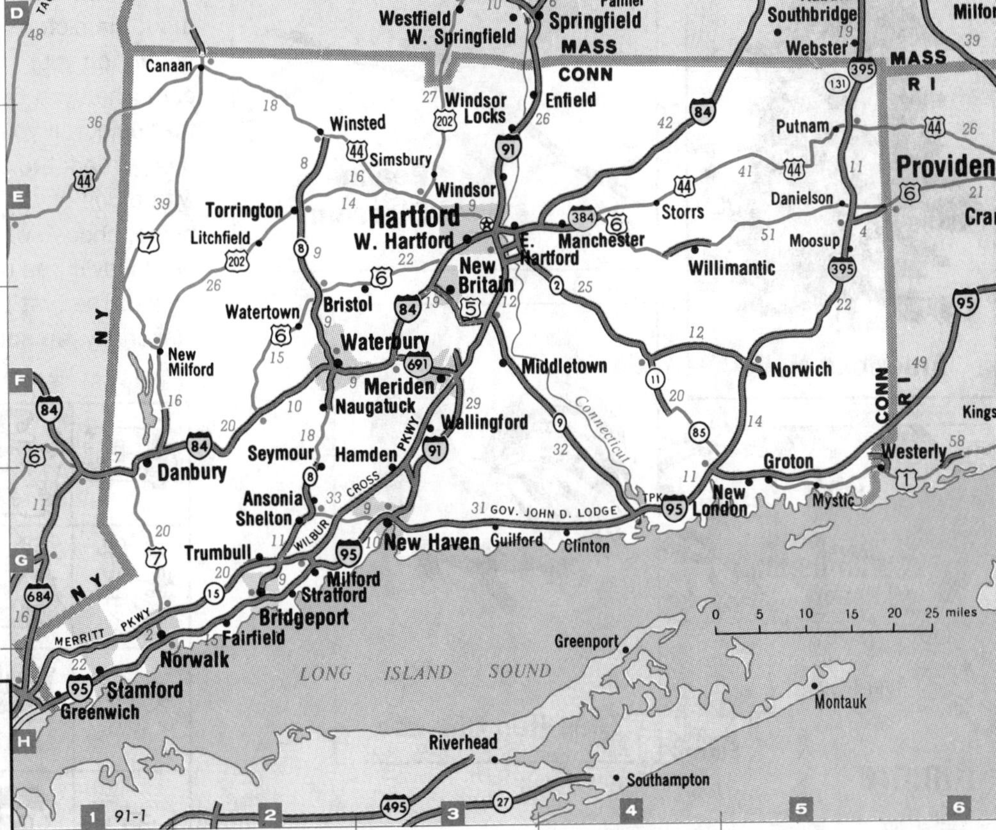

White Oak

Color by number
1 — Blue
2 — Red
3 — Green
4 — Yellow
5 — Brown
6 — Orange

DELAWARE

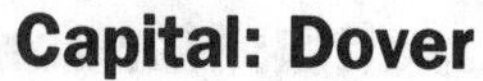

Capital: Dover

American Holly

Peach Blossom

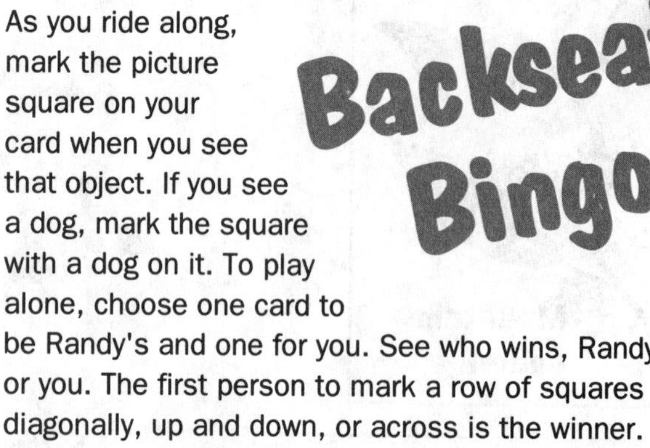

Backseat Bingo

As you ride along, mark the picture square on your card when you see that object. If you see a dog, mark the square with a dog on it. To play alone, choose one card to be Randy's and one for you. See who wins, Randy or you. The first person to mark a row of squares diagonally, up and down, or across is the winner.

Blue Hen Chicken

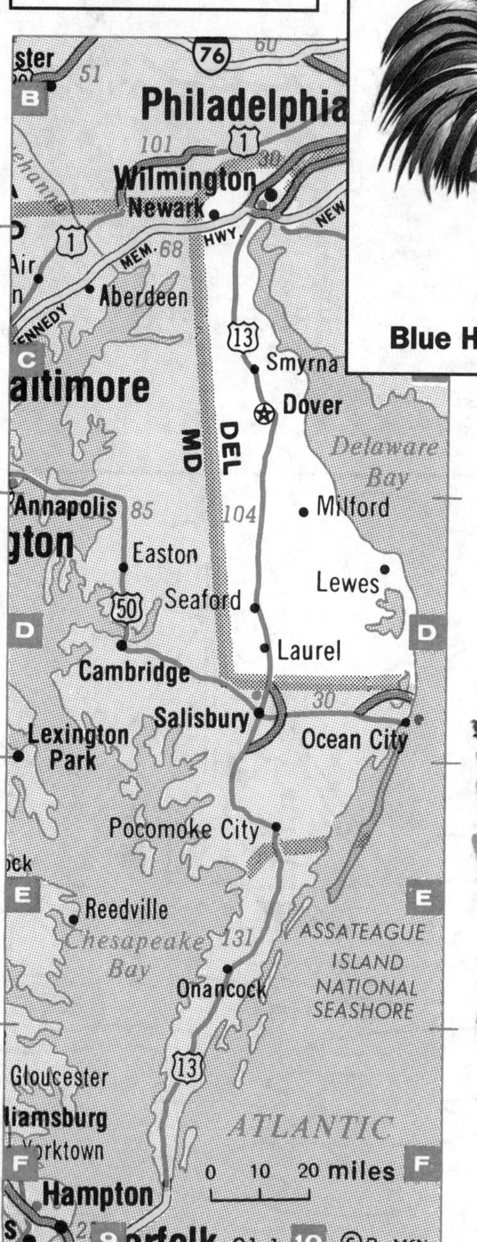

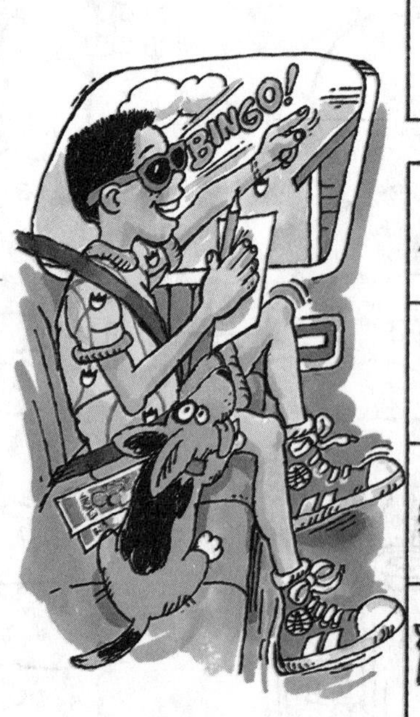

Sabal Palm

FLORIDA

Capital: Tallahassee

Orange Blossom

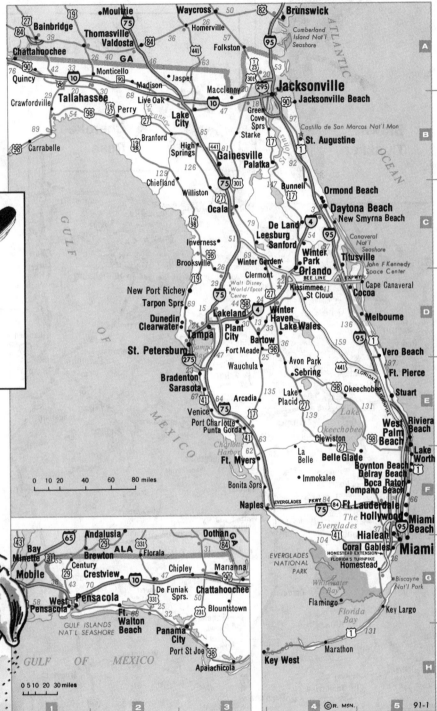

Mockingbird

Beachcombing

Explore the beach with Randy. Help him find the two seashells that are exactly alike.

GEORGIA

Capital: Atlanta

Brown Thrasher

Cherokee Rose

Live Oak

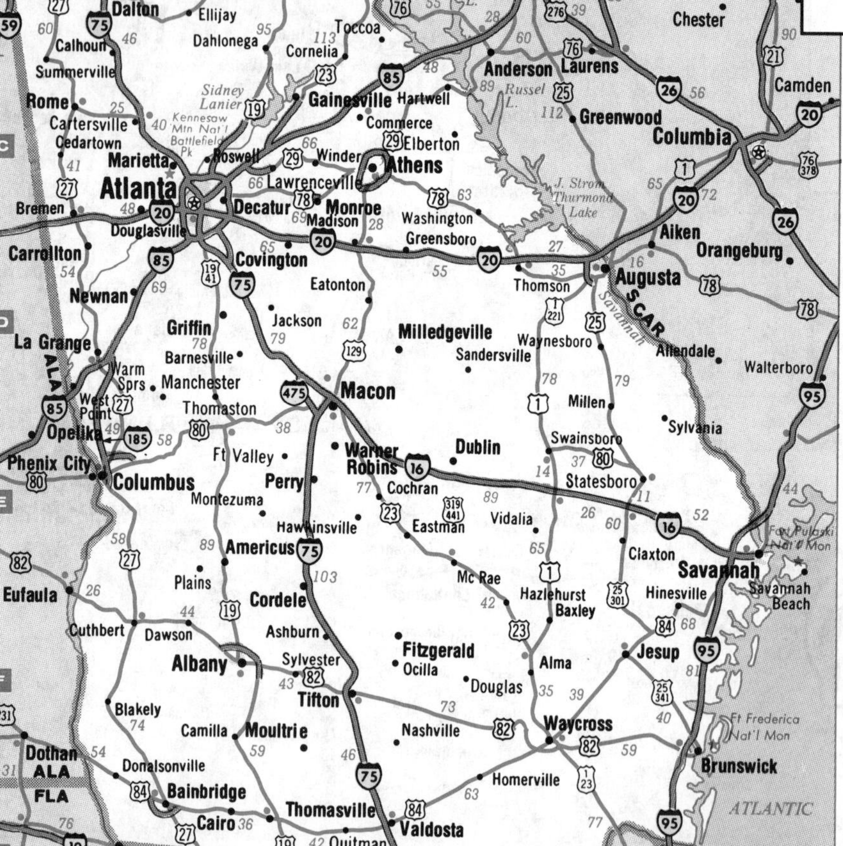

With a dark crayon color out every X, Y, and Z. The remaining letters will tell you and Randy what state this is, plus who are its neighbors.

N	X	Z	A	L	A	B	A	M	A	X	Y	A
Y	O	Y	X	Y	X	Y	Y	X	Z	Y	N	X
X	Z	R	Z	Y	Y	Z	X	Y	Y	I	Y	Z
G	Z	Y	T	X	Z	X	Z	X	L	Z	X	F
E	Y	X	Z	H	X	Z	Y	O	X	Y	X	L
O	Z	Y	Z	Y	C	Y	R	Y	Z	X	Y	O
R	Y	Z	X	Y	Z	A	Z	X	Y	Z	X	R
G	X	Y	Y	Z	C	X	R	Y	X	Z	Y	I
I	Y	Z	X	H	Y	Z	Y	O	Z	Y	X	D
A	Z	X	T	Z	Y	X	Z	Y	L	Y	Z	A
Z	X	U	Y	X	Z	Y	X	Y	X	I	Y	X
X	O	X	Z	Y	Z	X	Z	Z	X	Z	N	Z
S	X	T	E	N	N	E	S	S	E	E	Z	A

HAWAII

Capital: Honolulu

Hawaiian Goose

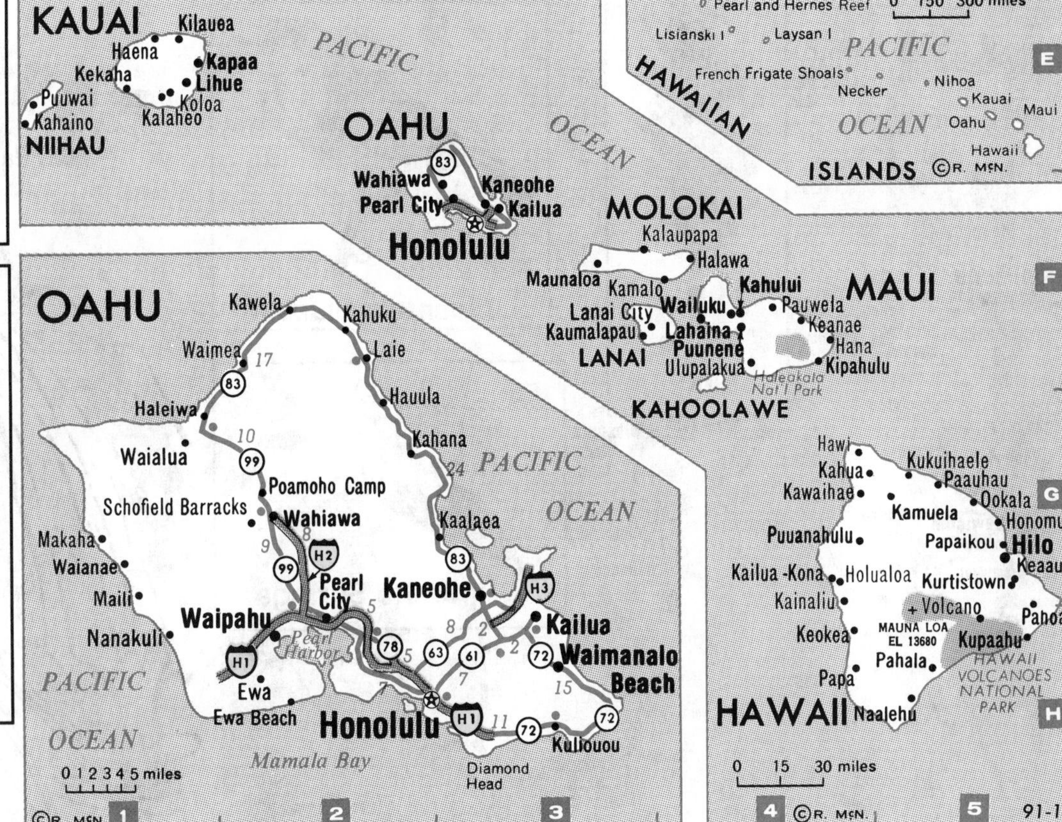

Candlenut

Hibiscus

KAUAI
Kilauea
Haena · Kapaa
Kekaha · Lihue
Puuwai · Koloa
Kahaino · Kalaheo
NIIHAU

OAHU
Wahiawa · Kaneohe
Pearl City · Kailua
Honolulu

PACIFIC

OCEAN

Pearl and Hernes Reef 0 150 300 miles
Lisianski I · Laysan I PACIFIC
HAWAIIAN French Frigate Shoals
Necker · Nihoa OCEAN
· Kauai
Oahu · Maui
ISLANDS ©R. M§N. Hawaii

MOLOKAI
Kalaupapa
Halawa
Maunaloa · Kamalo Kahului MAUI
Lanai City Wailuku · Pauwela
Kaumalapau Lahaina · Keanae
LANAI Puunene Hana
Ulupalakua Kipahulu
Haleakala Nat'l Park
KAHOOLAWE

OAHU
Kawela · Kahuku
Waimea 17 Laie
83 Hauula
Haleiwa Kahana
10
Waialua 24 PACIFIC
99 Poamoho Camp
Schofield Barracks · Wahiawa OCEAN
9 Kaalaea
Makaha H2 83
Waianae 99 · Pearl City · Kaneohe
Maili H3
Waipahu Kailua
Nanakuli Pearl Harbor 8 2 Waimanalo Beach
PACIFIC 78 63 61 72
H1 5 2
OCEAN Ewa 7 15
Ewa Beach Honolulu H1 11 72 72
Mamala Bay Diamond Kuliouou
Head
0 1 2 3 4 5 miles ©R. M§N. 1 2 3

Hawi Kukuihaele
Kahua Paauhau
Kawaihae Ookala
Puuanahulu Kamuela Honomu
Papaikou Hilo
Kailua -Kona Keaau
Kainaliu Holualoa Kurtistown
Keokea + Volcano Pahoa
MAUNA LOA Kupaahu
EL 13680
Papa Pahala HAWAII
VOLCANOES
NATIONAL
HAWAII Naalehu PARK
0 15 30 miles
4 ©R. M§N. 5 91-1

Aloha!

Find these Hawaiian places and things.

ash
candlenut
canoe
crater
Haleakala
Hawaii
hibiscus

Honolulu
hula
Kauai
Kilauea
Kona
Lanai

lava
lei
luau
Maui
Mauna
Kea

Mauna Loa
Molokai
nene (goose)
Nihau
nut
Oahu

outrigger
palm
sand
shell
surf
tree

M	A	U	N	A	L	O	A	I	U	A	M
A	K	S	S	A	A	V	A	L	A	O	J
U	A	H	H	O	N	O	L	U	L	U	A
N	U	E	A	F	A	O	A	O	U	T	T
A	A	L	W	R	I	S	K	Q	H	R	U
K	I	L	A	U	E	A	A	U	U	I	N
E	D	E	I	S	I	N	E	A	A	G	E
A	T	I	I	M	E	D	L	H	U	G	L
E	R	M	O	L	O	K	A	I	L	E	D
N	E	O	N	A	C	T	H	N	O	R	N
E	E	U	H	P	R	E	T	A	R	C	A
N	T	U	H	I	B	I	S	C	U	S	C

IDAHO

Capital: Boise

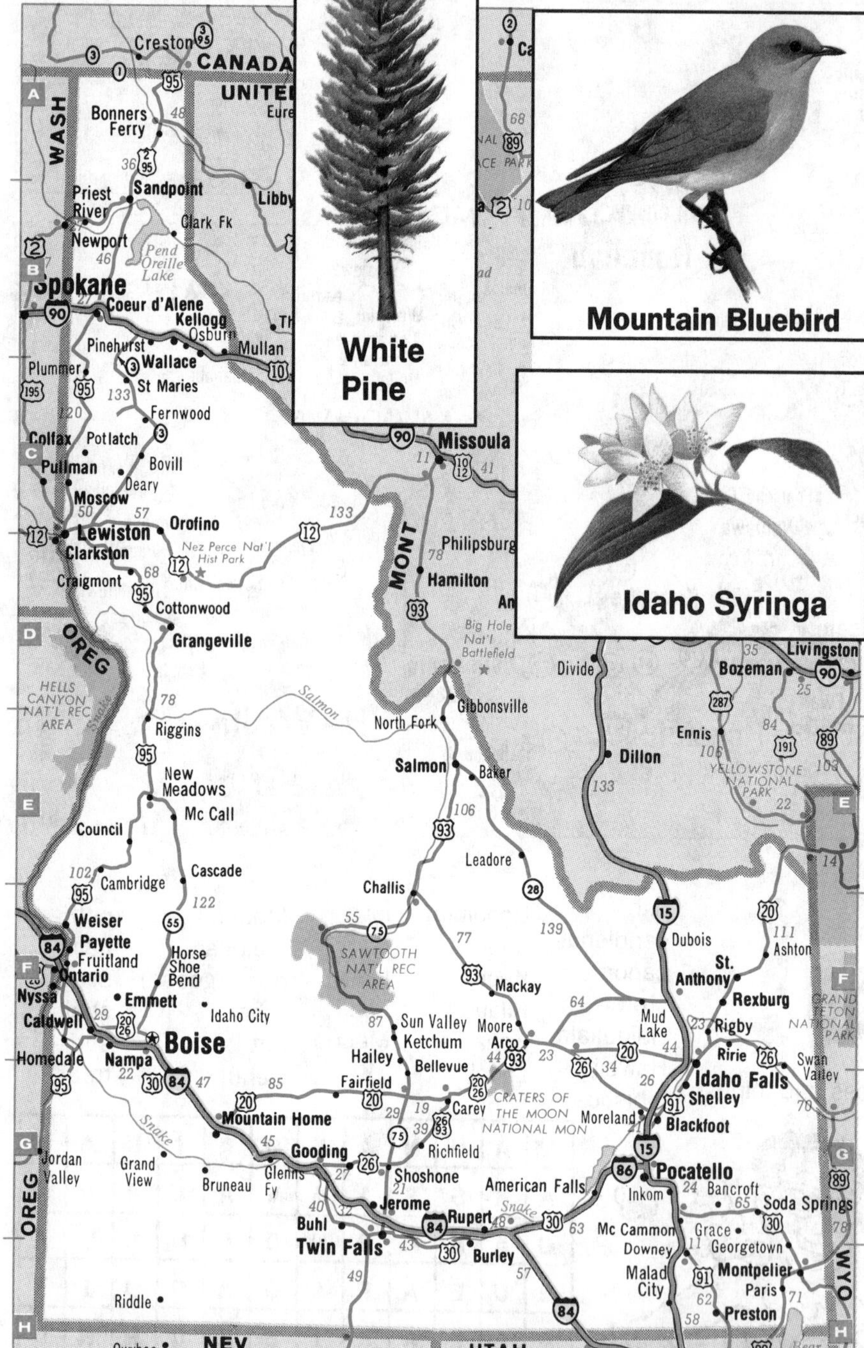

White Pine

Mountain Bluebird

Idaho Syringa

Gone Fishin'

Did Randy catch the fish?

ILLINOIS

Capital: Springfield

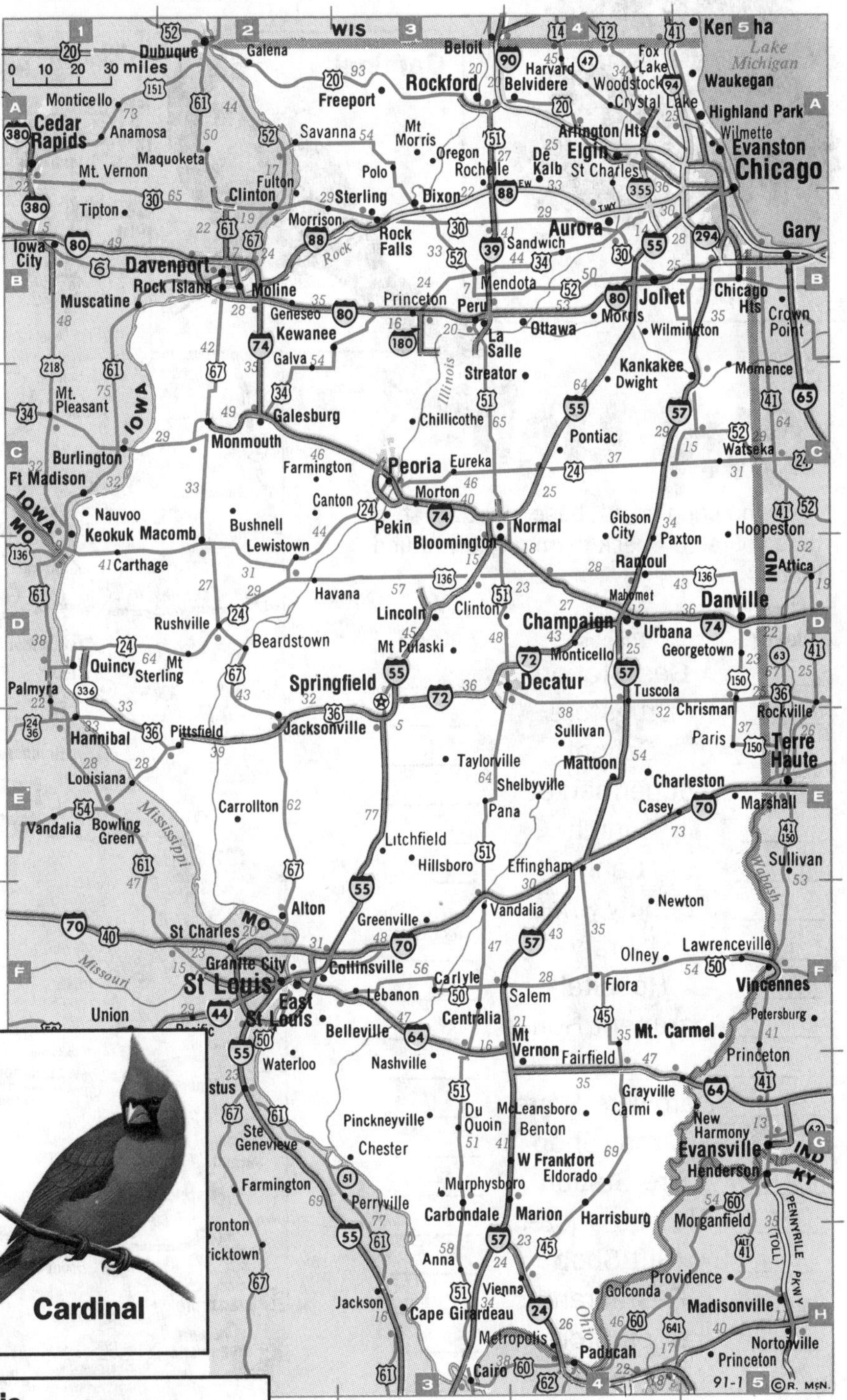

Unscramble all the letters of the same color (type) to find six things about Illinois.

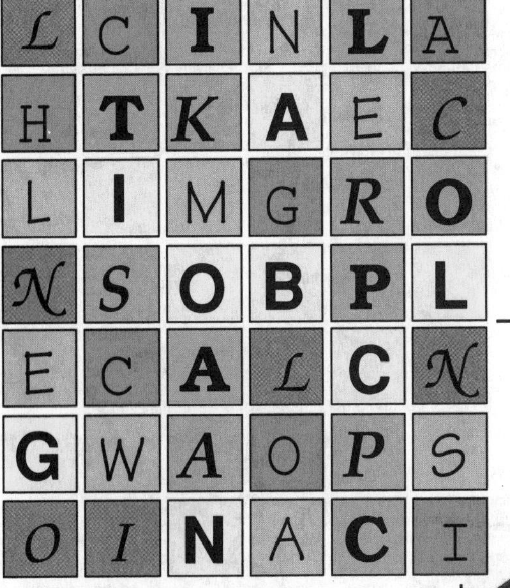

L	C	I	N	L	A
H	T	K	A	E	C
L	I	M	G	R	O
N	S	O	B	P	L
E	C	A	L	C	N
G	W	A	O	P	S
O	I	N	A	C	I

Cardinal

White Oak

Illinois Native Violet

Tulip Poplar

INDIANA

Capital: Indianapolis

Cardinal

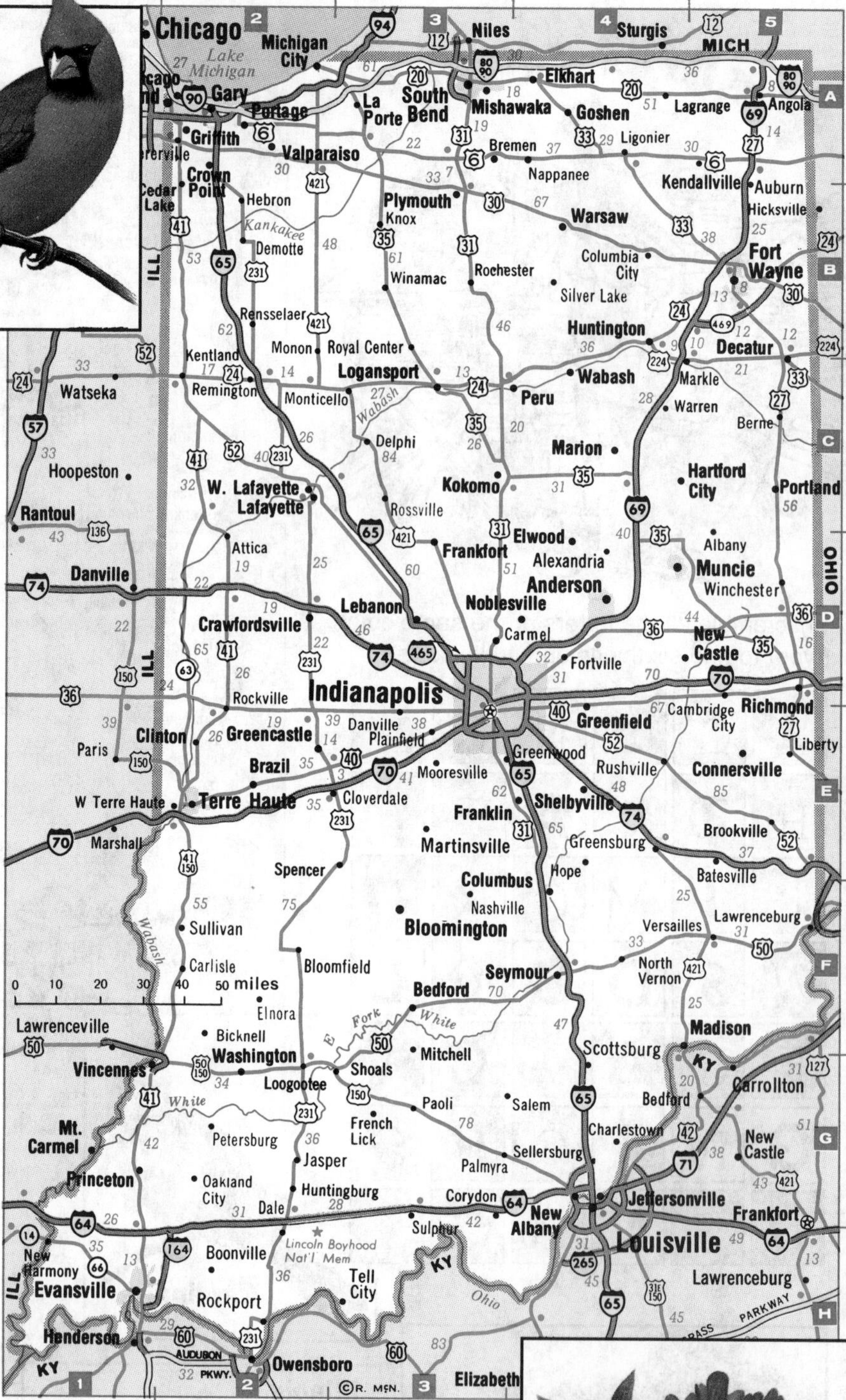

City Lights!

See who can find all these places first, or time yourself. Check them off as you find them.

First Player	Places	Second Player
______	Gas Station	______
______	Drugstore	______
______	School	______
______	Supermarket	______
______	Church	______
______	Bank	______
______	Beauty Shop	______
______	Library	______
______	Hospital	______
______	Apartment House	______
______	Garage	______
______	Hardware Store	______
______	Barber Shop	______
______	Fire Station	______
______	Hotel or Motel	______
______	Gift Shop	______
______	Restaurant	______
______	Book Store	______
______	Pet Shop	______
______	Movie Theater	______
______	Police Station	______
______	Auto Dealer	______
______	Bakery	______
______	Toy Store	______
______	Pizzeria	______
______	Florist	______

Peony

IOWA

Capital: Des Moines

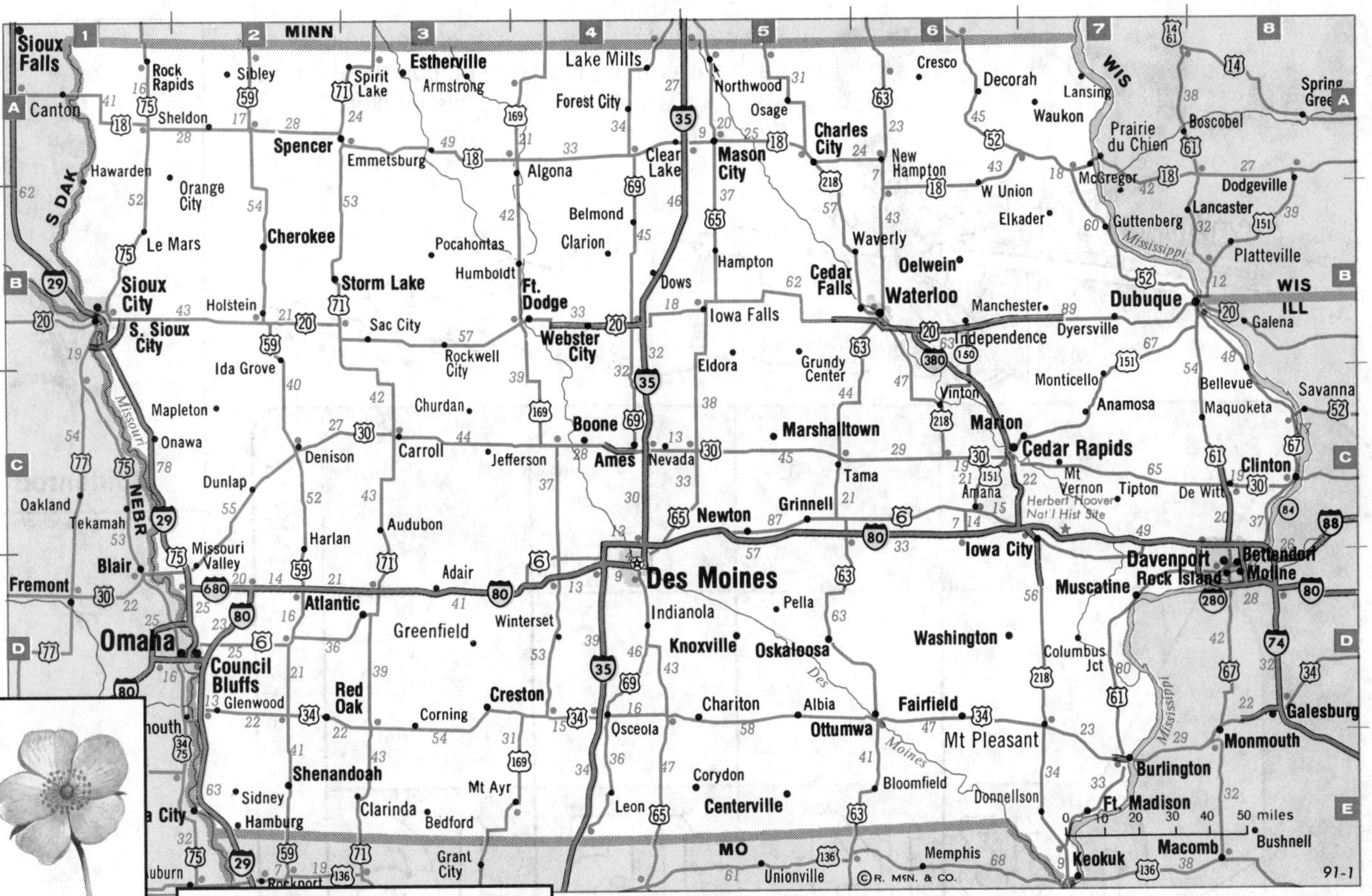

Wild Rose

Eastern Goldfinch

Oak

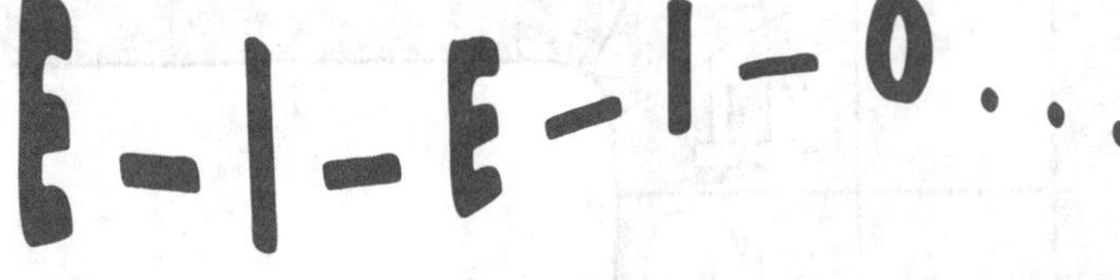

Study for one minute these things you would see on a farm. Close the book. See how many you can remember.

KENTUCKY

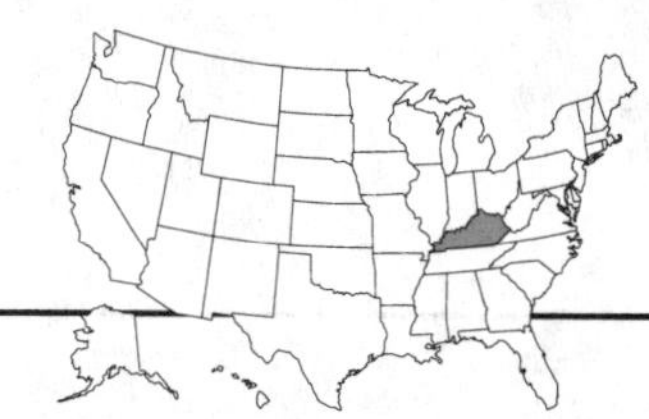

Capital: Frankfort

Go For It!

Three can play. Use coins or other markers. Each player must find each number in turn on a license plate; then move up his marker. The first to reach the finish line wins.

Goldenrod

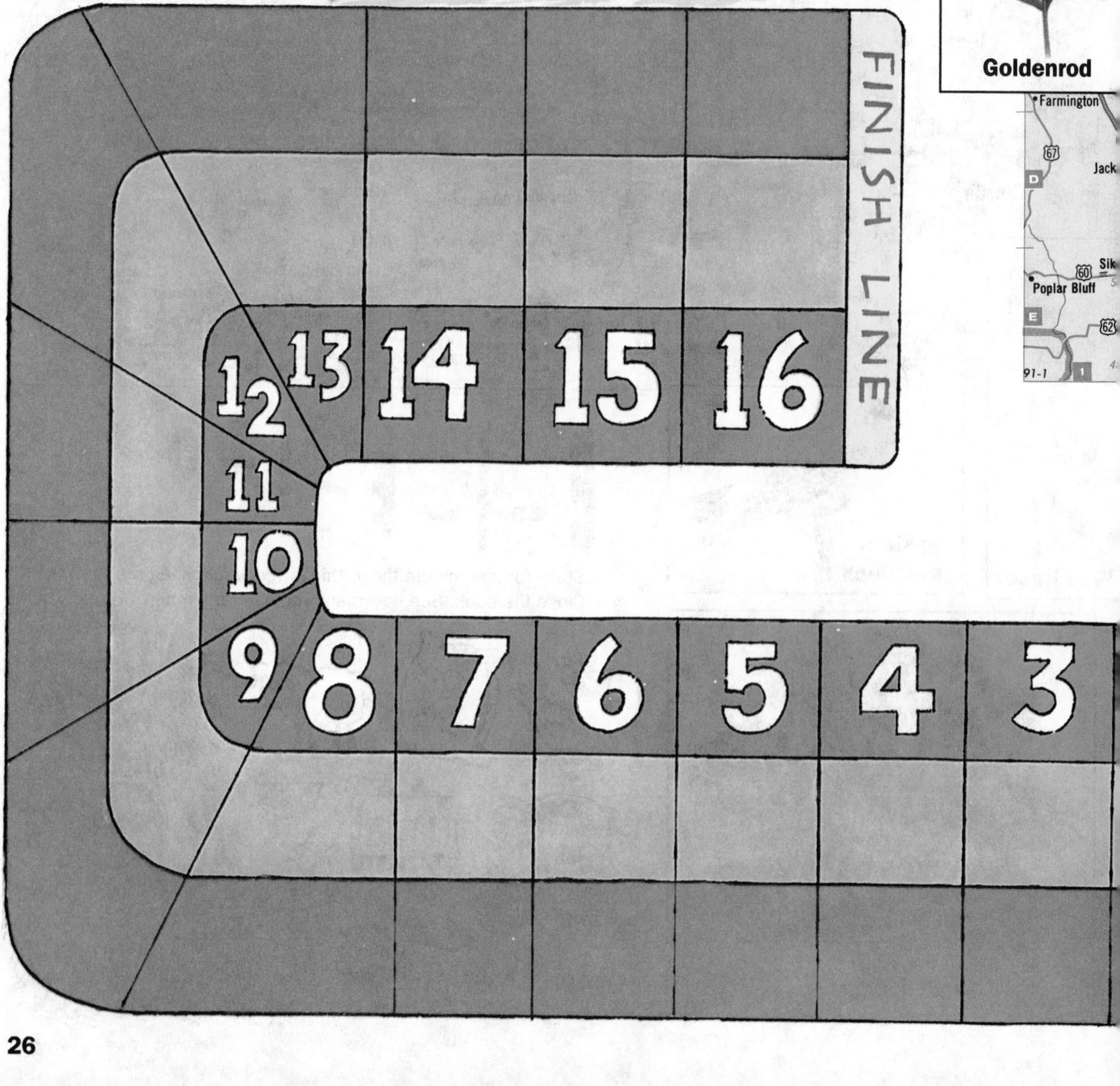

FINISH LINE

16 15 14 13 12 11 10 9 8 7 6 5 4 3

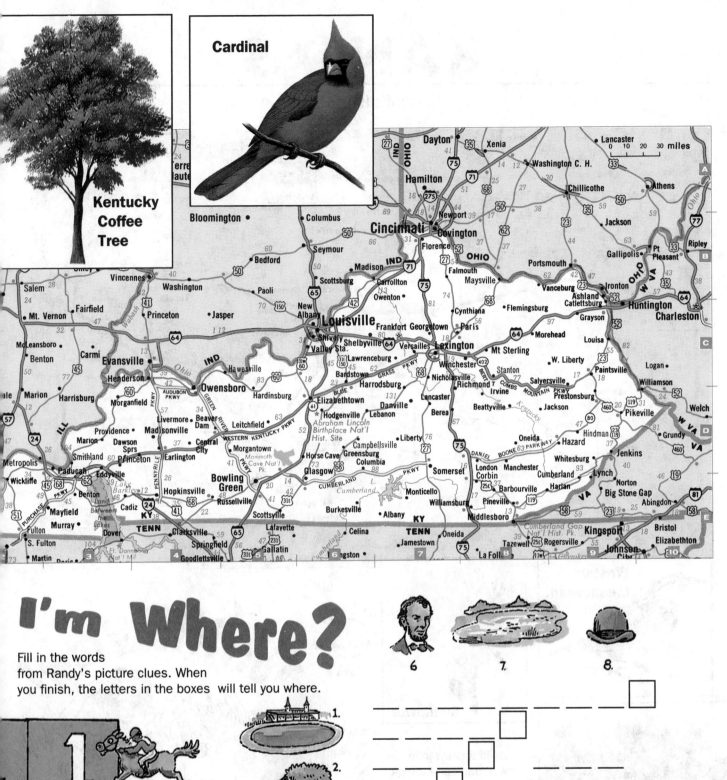

Kentucky Coffee Tree

Cardinal

I'm Where?

Fill in the words from Randy's picture clues. When you finish, the letters in the boxes will tell you where.

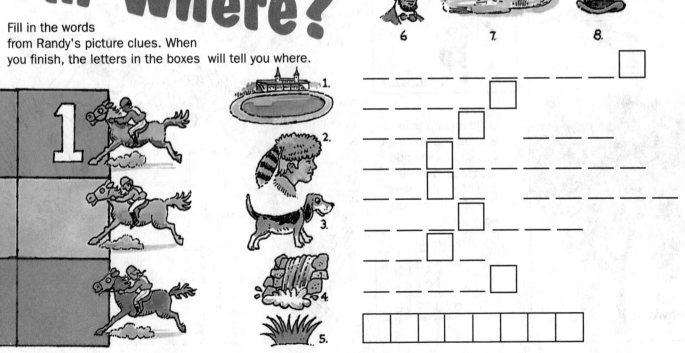

1\. 2. 3. 4. 5. 6 7. 8.

KANSAS

Capital: Topeka

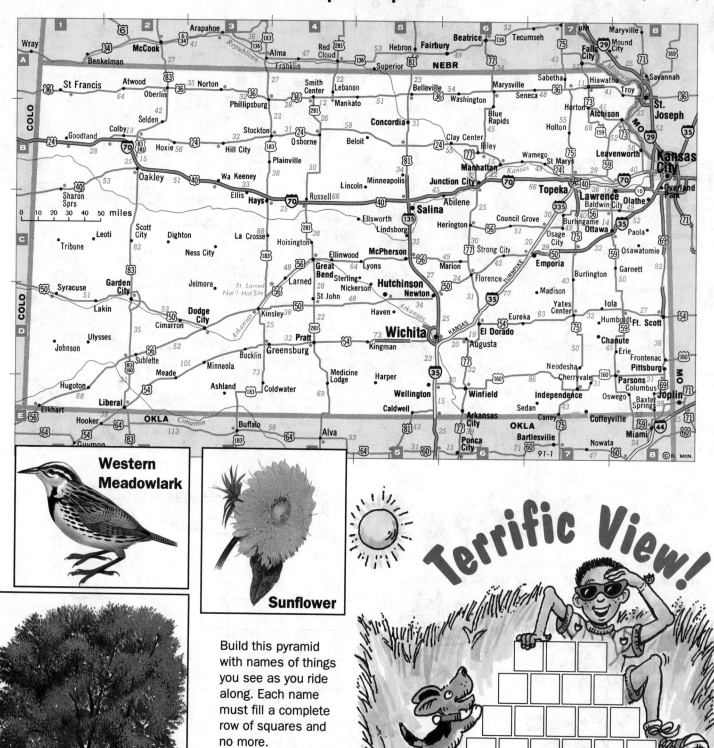

Western Meadowlark

Sunflower

Cottonwood

Terrific View!

Build this pyramid with names of things you see as you ride along. Each name must fill a complete row of squares and no more.

Example

M	A	N

D	U	C	K

H	O	U	S	E

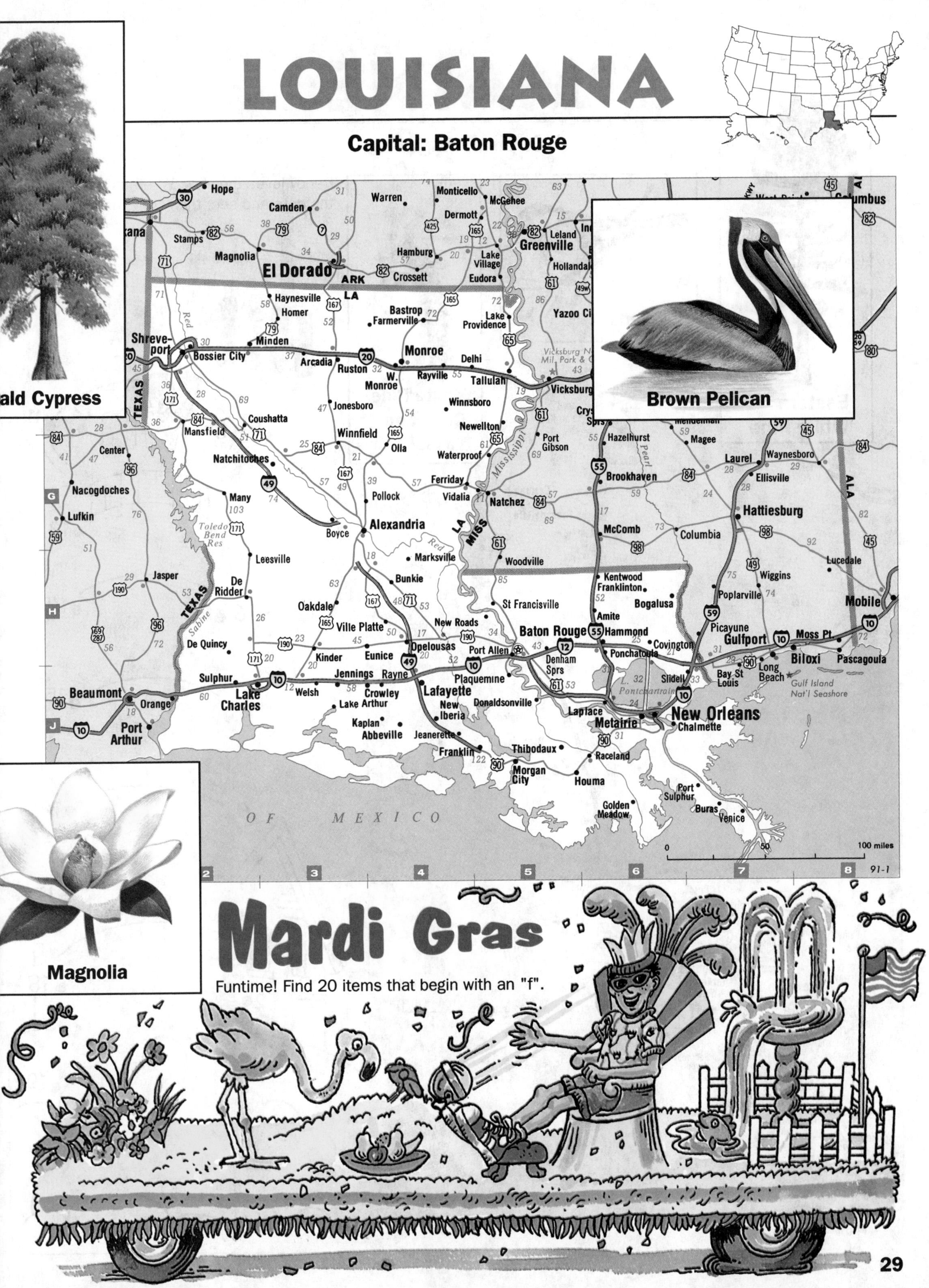

LOUISIANA
Capital: Baton Rouge
Bald Cypress
Brown Pelican
Magnolia
Shreveport
Bossier City
Monroe
Alexandria
Lafayette
Lake Charles
Baton Rouge
New Orleans
Metairie
Houma
OF MEXICO
TEXAS
ARK
LA
MISS
100 miles
Mardi Gras
Funtime! Find 20 items that begin with an "f".

MAINE

Capital: Augusta

Eastern
White Pine

Chickadee

White Pine
Cone and
Tassel

Randy loves the view. Where is he? Connect
the dots and see, then color the picture.

Hi!

10

9 8 12 11

7 13

6 14

5 15

4 16

3 17

2 18

1 19

Map labels

Edmundston
Madawaska
QUE N B
19
Fort Kent
Van Buren
185
St. A.
du Beaupre
Allagash
Eagle Lake
22
St. Pamphile
20
Montmagny
Levis-Lauzon
Caribou
Fort Fairfield
Presque Isle
Ashland
90
173 104
Mars Hill
56
Beauceville
Ville St. Georges
Chamberlain Lake
Hartland
CANADA UNITED STATES
95 16
95 Woodstock
Patten
11
Houlton
44
Moosehead Lake
201
40 69 1
Jackman
2 MT 2
Lac Megantic
42 56
Millinocket
Danforth
Vanceboro
Greenville
28 Mattawamkeag
75 24
Brownville Jct
Lincoln
Stratton
Dover-Foxcroft
Howland
37
St Stephan
Guilford
46
Calais
Bingham
33 21
Kingfield
Dexter
2
Rangeley
Old Town
Eastport
Newport
Orono
Madison
201 50 Bangor
Skowhegan 52 Brewer
Machias 60
Lubec
35 14 Pittsfield
Farmington
2 Hampden 26
Mexico
Fairfield 202 1 Bucksport
40
Bethel Rumford 22 34 99 1
Waterville Ellsworth Milbridge
Livermore Falls 95 Winslow Belfast
Winthrop Searsport Bar Harbor
Norway 202 29 Augusta Camden ACADIA NAT'L PARK
Lewiston 33 Gardiner
Auburn Waldoboro 91 Camden
Fryeburg 50 TPK Rockland
14 495 Bath Thomaston
N Windham 25 Wiscasset
Cornish 30 Brunswick
Westbrook Yarmouth Boothbay Harbor
70 Portland
Sanford 202 Old Orchard Beach
46 Saco
Rochester Biddeford
Kennebunk
95 Ogunquit
4 Dover York Beach
Kittery
Portsmouth
Newburyport

ATLANTIC OCEAN

Acadia Nat'l Park

0 10 20 30 40 50 miles

30

MARYLAND

Capital: Annapolis

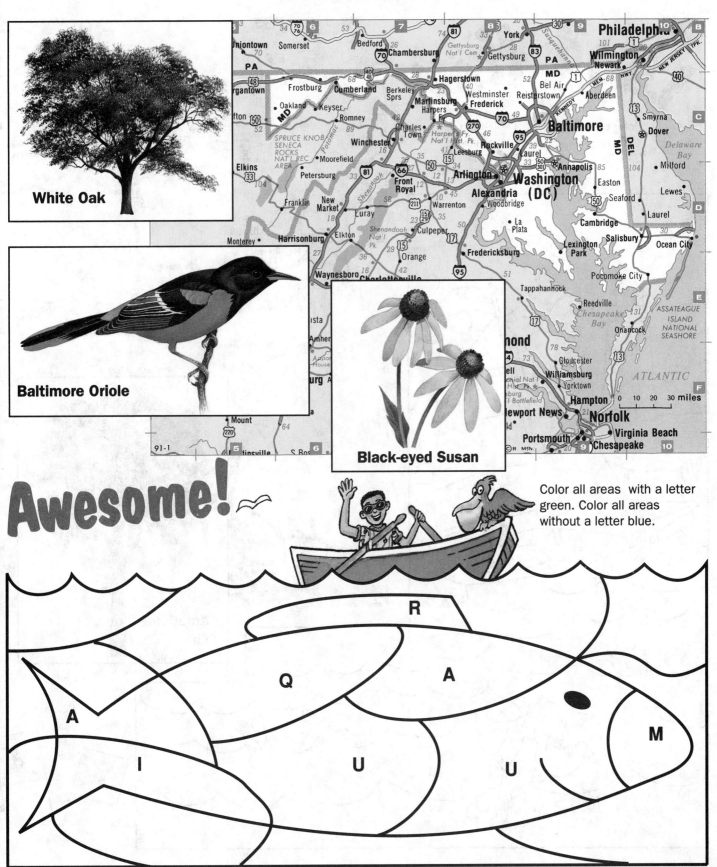

White Oak

Baltimore Oriole

Black-eyed Susan

Awesome!

Color all areas with a letter green. Color all areas without a letter blue.

MASSACHUSETTS

Capital: Boston

Land Ho!

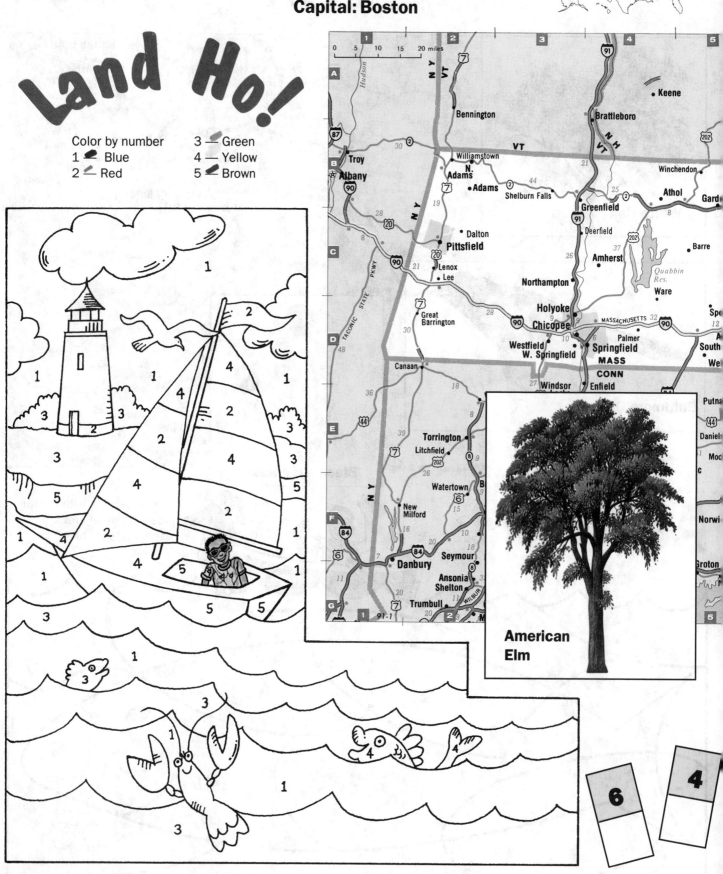

Color by number
1 — Blue
2 — Red
3 — Green
4 — Yellow
5 — Brown

Bennington
Keene
Brattleboro
Troy
Albany
Williamstown
N. Adams
Adams
Shelburn Falls
Winchendon
Athol
Greenfield
Deerfield
Dalton
Pittsfield
Lenox
Lee
Amherst
Barre
Quabbin Res.
Northampton
Ware
Great Barrington
Holyoke
Chicopee
Westfield
W. Springfield
Springfield
Palmer
MASS
CONN
Canaan
Windsor
Enfield
Torrington
Litchfield
Watertown
New Milford
Danbury
Seymour
Ansonia
Shelton
Trumbull
TACONIC STATE PKWY
MASSACHUSETTS

American Elm

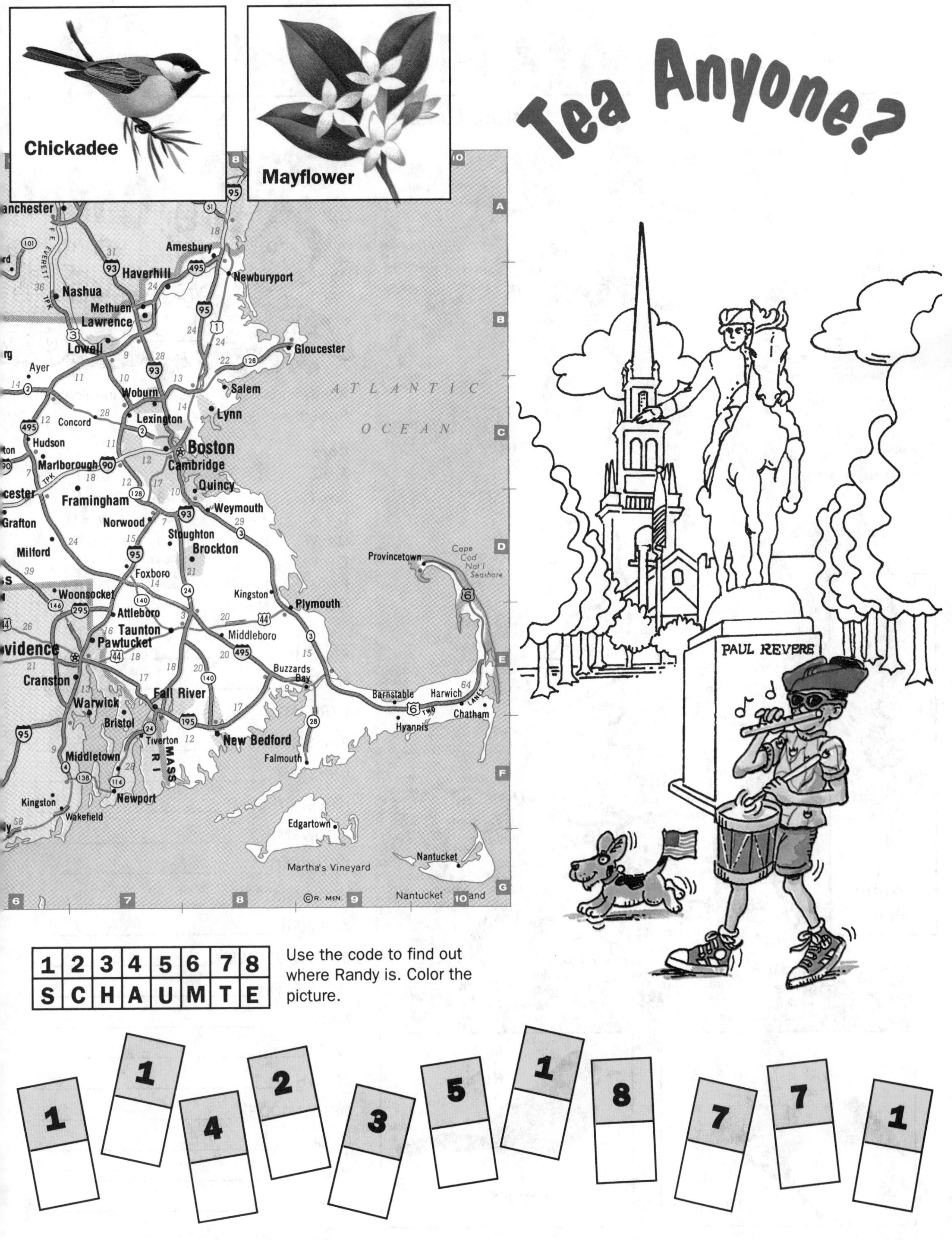
Tea Anyone?
Chickadee
Mayflower
Manchester
Amesbury
Haverhill
Newburyport
Nashua
Methuen
Lawrence
Lowell
Gloucester
Ayer
Woburn
Salem
Lexington
Lynn
ATLANTIC OCEAN
Concord
Hudson
Boston
Marlborough
Cambridge
Quincy
Framingham
Weymouth
Grafton
Norwood
Stoughton
Brockton
Milford
Provincetown
Cape Cod Nat'l Seashore
Foxboro
Woonsocket
Kingston
Plymouth
Attleboro
Taunton
Pawtucket
Middleboro
Cranston
Buzzards Bay
Warwick
Fall River
Barnstable
Harwich
Chatham
Bristol
Hyannis
Tiverton
New Bedford
Middletown
Falmouth
R I
MASS
Kingston
Newport
Wakefield
Edgartown
Nantucket
Martha's Vineyard
©R. McN.
Nantucket Island
PAUL REVERE
| 1 | 2 | 3 | 4 | 5 | 6 | 7 | 8 |
| S | C | H | A | U | M | T | E |
Use the code to find out where Randy is. Color the picture.
1 1 4 2 3 5 1 8 7 7 1

MICHIGAN

Capital: Lansing

White Pine

Apple Blossom

Robin

Crack the Code!

Randy knows what's happening in Michigan. Solve his code to see.

Code:

A = Z	H = S	O = L	U = F
B = Y	I = R	P = K	V = E
C = X	J = Q	Q = J	W = D
D = W	K = P	R = I	X = C
E = V	L = O	S = H	Y = B
F = U	M = N	T = G	Z = A
G = T	N = M		

SRPRMT ______________________

HPRRMT ______________________

HZRORMT ______________________

ILXP SFMGRMT ______________________

URHSRMT ______________________

HMLDNLYRORMT ______________________

XZMLVRMT ______________________

HSLKKRMT ______________________

HDRNNRMT ______________________

XZNKRMT ______________________

SLIHVYZXP IRWRMT ______________________

NRMV GLFIH ______________________

NFHVFNH ______________________

KZIPH ______________________

WFMVH ______________________

DRMWNROOH ______________________

ULIGH ______________________

HLL OLXPH ______________________

ALLH ______________________

YVZXSVH ______________________

MINNESOTA

Capital: St. Paul

Red Pine

Common Loon

Pink-and-white Lady's Slipper

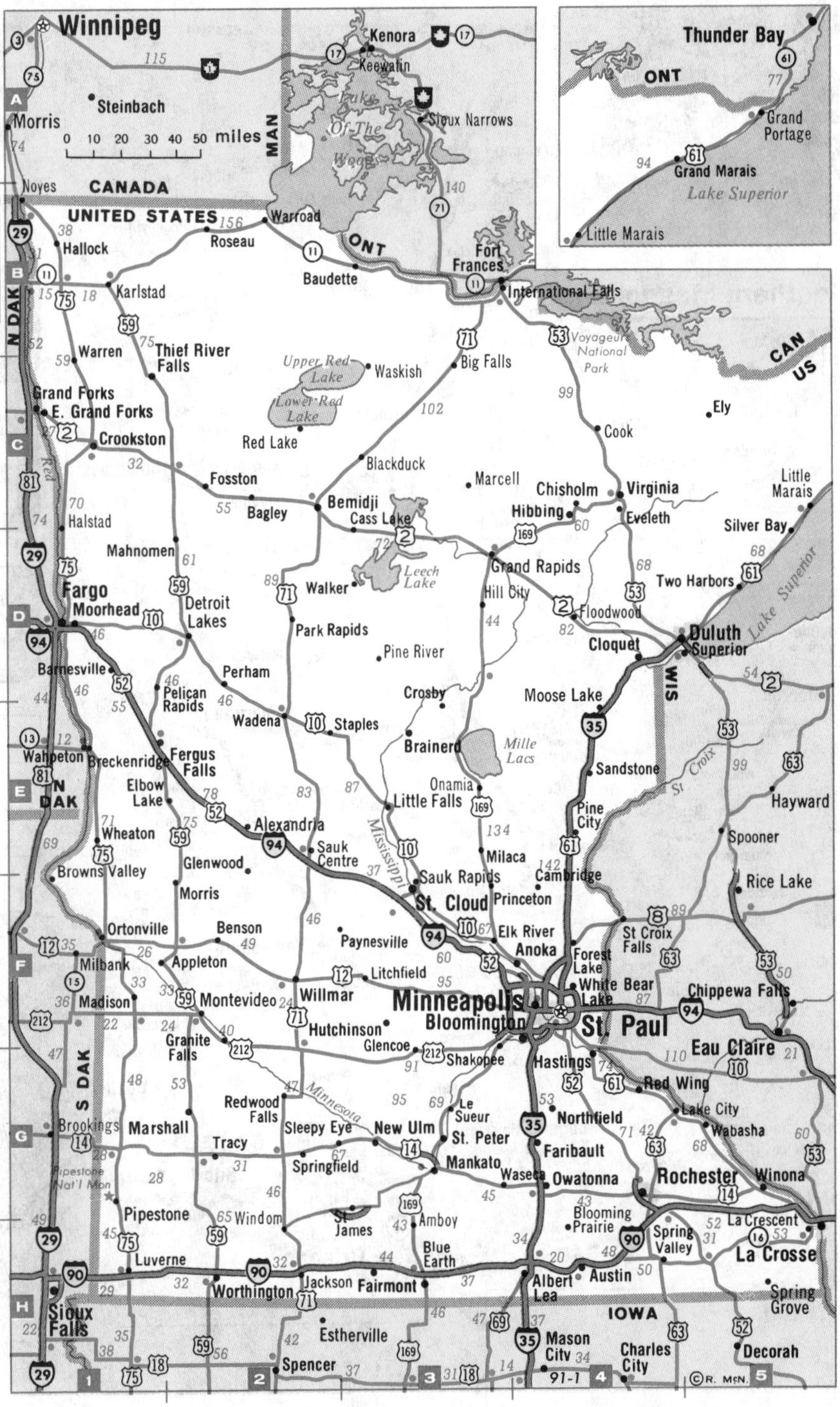

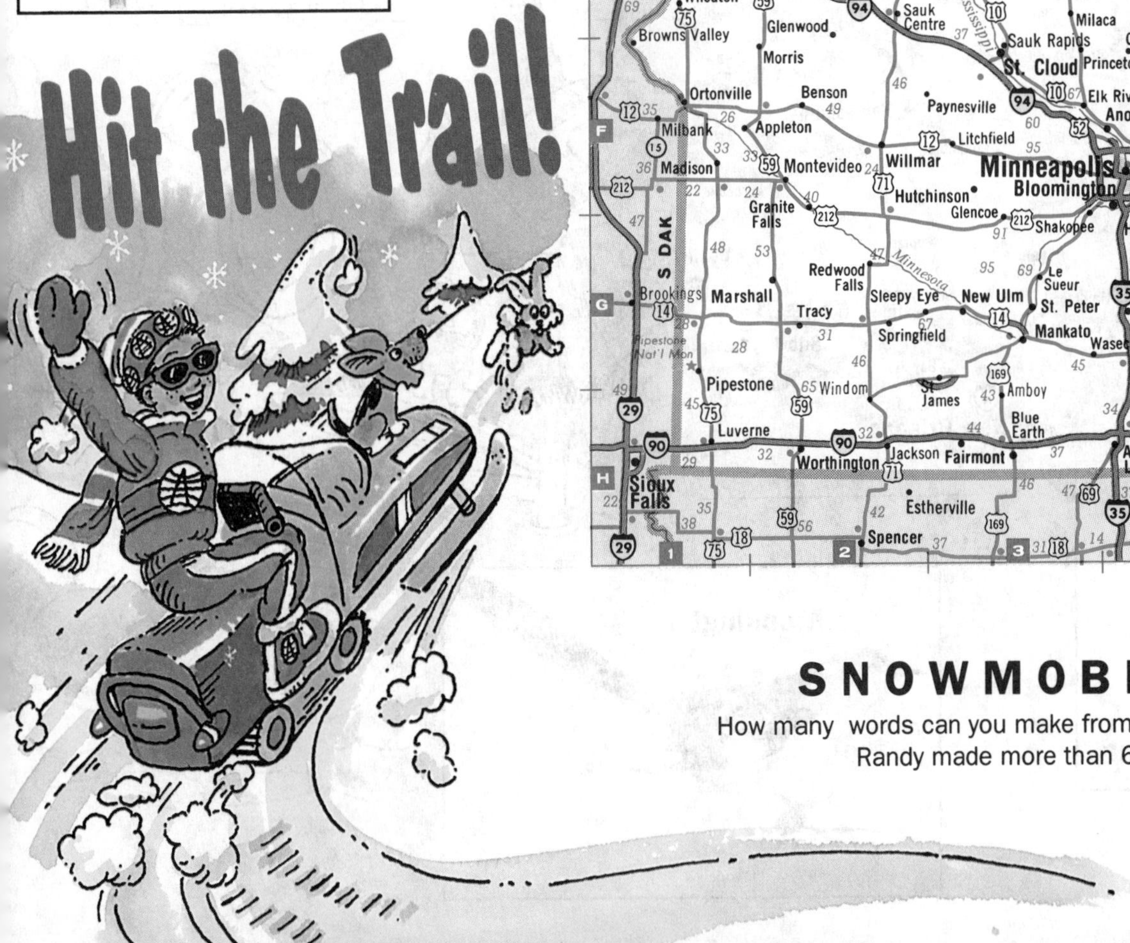

SNOWMOBILE

How many words can you make from these letters?
Randy made more than 60.

MISSISSIPPI

Capital: Jackson

Sign Language!

Match the sign with its meaning.

1 2 3

4 5 6

7 8 9

☐	Picnic Site	☐	Swimming	☐	Campground
☐	First Aid	☐	Hiking Trail	☐	Playground
☐	Information	☐	Fishing	☐	Horse Trail

Southern Magnolia

Magnolia

Mockingbird

MISSOURI

Capital: Jefferson City

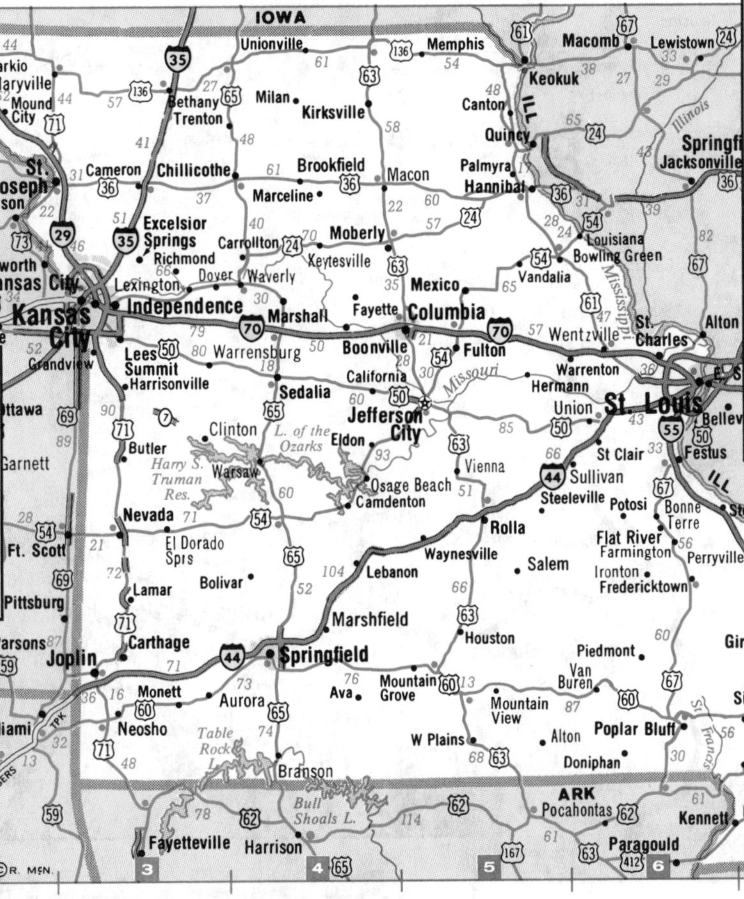

Bluebird

Dogwood

Hawthorn

Look At That!

automobile	corn	garden	pail	sign
barn	cow	golfcourse	picnic	silo
beach	crow	highway	pigs	stop
bike	dog	hill	pony	stores
boat	ducks	home	river	tire
bridge	farm	horse	road	town
bus	fence	lake	rock	tractor
cab	ferry	maps	sale	train
cat	flowers	mountain	sand	tree
chicken	forest	ocean	sheep	windmill

Find and circle these travel sights.

D	A	O	R	L	S	E	A	F	E	E	N	R	W
U	E	A	O	A	N	N	E	L	R	C	R	E	I
C	H	I	C	K	E	N	I	R	I	N	O	V	N
K	B	I	K	E	M	B	O	A	T	E	C	I	D
S	U	A	S	T	O	R	E	S	R	F	A	R	M
N	S	D	R	M	H	I	H	S	A	T	A	C	I
E	S	P	O	N	Y	D	I	P	N	P	A	I	L
D	L	T	O	W	N	G	O	U	P	E	P	N	L
R	U	A	O	A	N	E	O	G	Y	E	I	C	I
A	T	R	S	P	A	M	Y	A	W	H	G	I	H
G	O	L	F	C	O	U	R	S	E	S	S	P	O
O	L	I	S	R	A	T	R	A	C	T	O	R	R
N	A	E	C	O	W	B	E	A	C	H	I	P	S
S	S	R	E	W	O	L	F	O	R	E	S	T	E

MONTANA

Capital: Helena

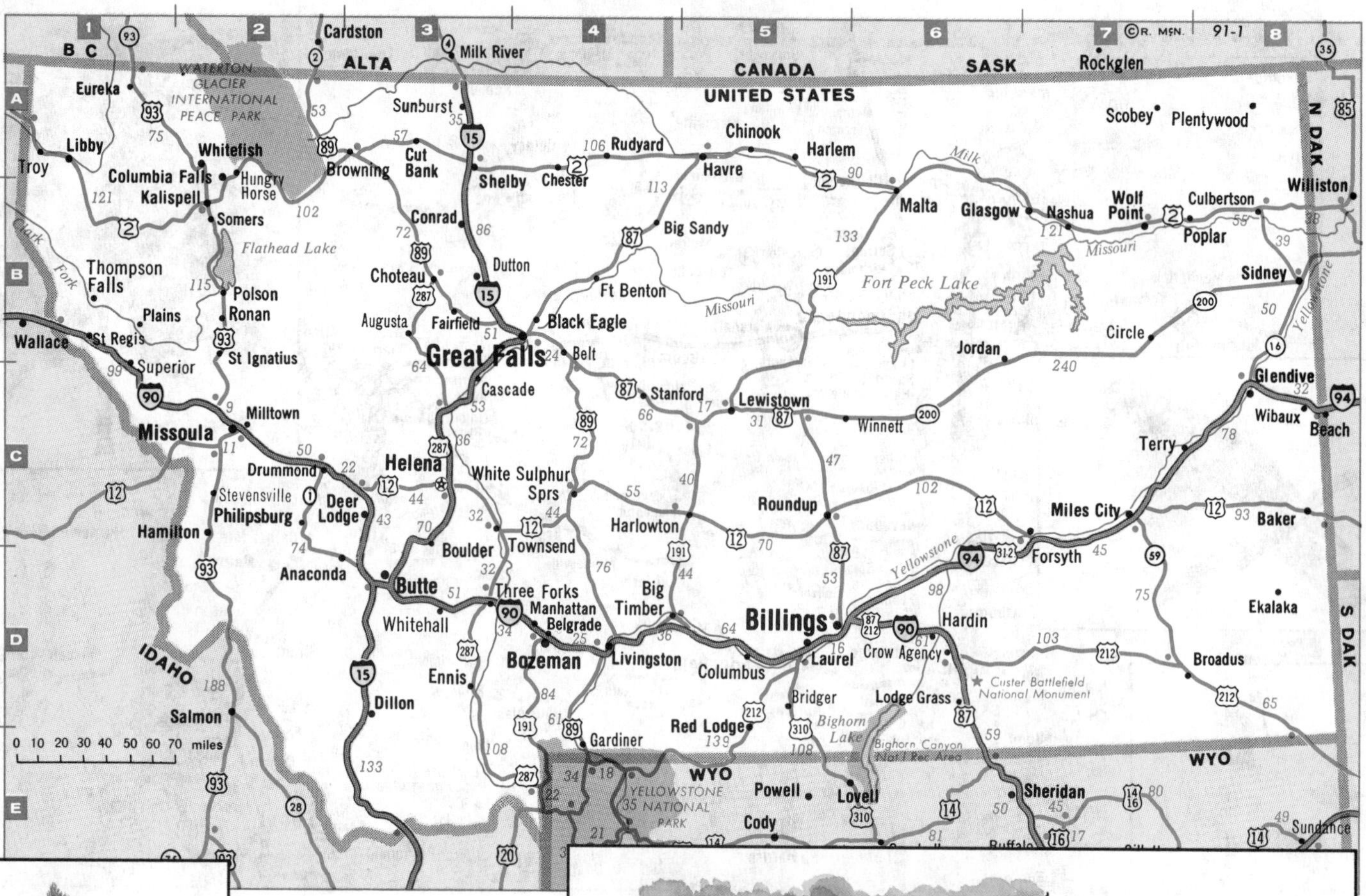

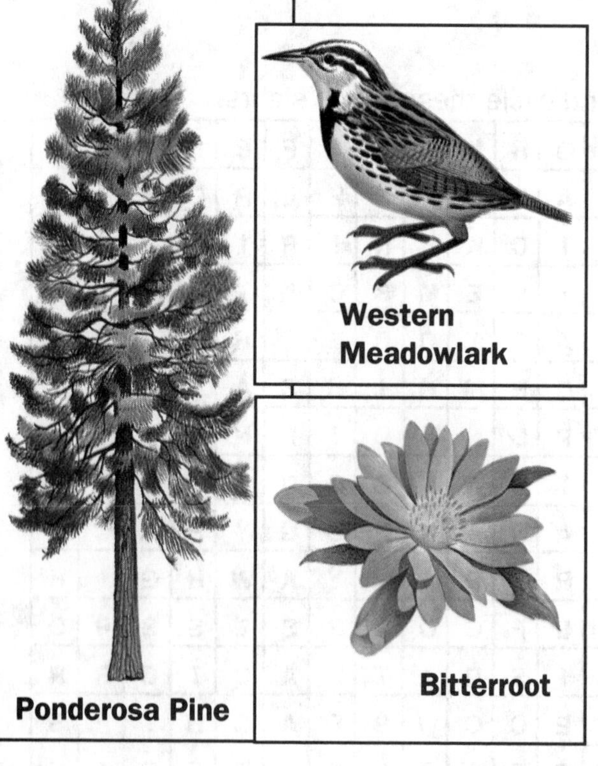

Ponderosa Pine

Western Meadowlark

Bitterroot

Help!

Help Randy unscramble the names of these wild babies; then match each baby with its parent.

1. bear	___ elwot
2. frog	___ cegytn
3. fox	___ niglsog
4. deer	___ tki
5. bobcat	___ malb
6. owl	___ pletado
7. sheep	___ buc
8. eagle	___ telage
9. swan	___ tikten
10. goose	___ wafn

NEBRASKA

Capital: Lincoln

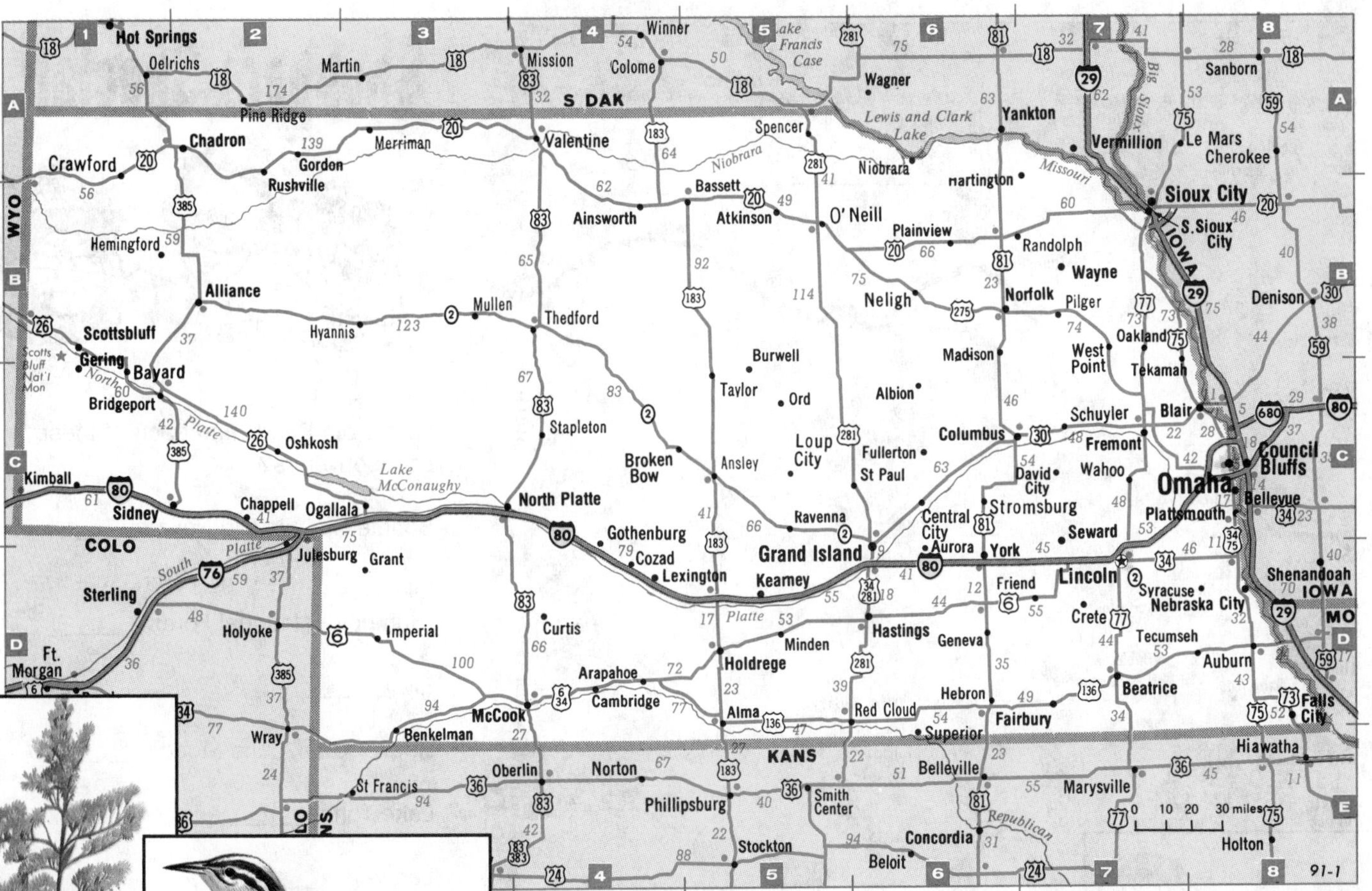

Goldenrod

Western Meadowlark

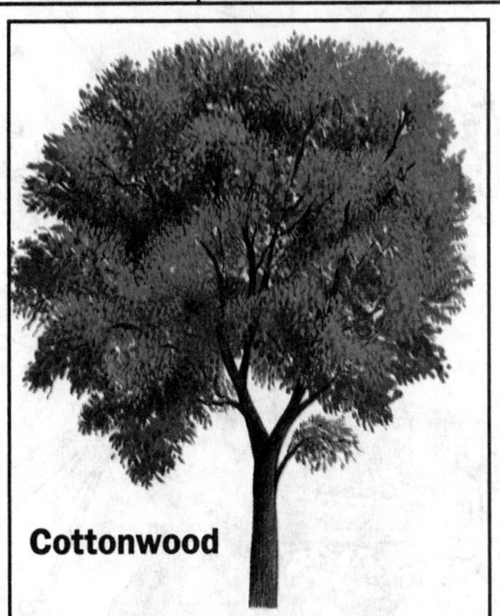

Cottonwood

Randy's Riddles

Help Randy find the hidden states.

Oh, what did Della wear? She wore a new jersey!
What did Mrs. sip? She sipped a mini soda!
How did Flora die? She died of misery!
Oh, where has Orie gone? She's gone where Michi's gone!
How did Wiscon sin? She stole a new brass key!
What did Tenne see? She saw what Arkan saw!
What did Io weigh? She weighed a washing ton!
And what did Ida hoe? She hoed a merry land!

NEVADA

Capital: Carson City

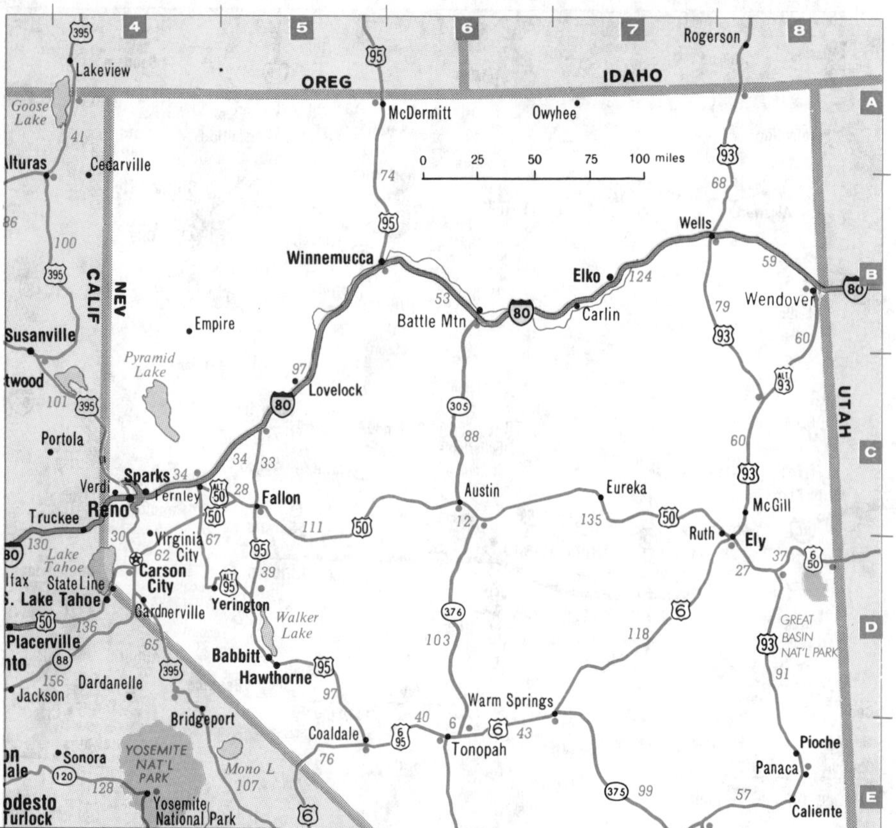

Shoppers Special!

Where did Randy find each of these cool souvenirs?

Bonnie Springs Old Nevada _____

Elko
(Humboldt National Forest) _____

Ely ______

Hoover Dam/Lake Mead ______

Lake Tahoe ______

Las Vegas ______

Reno ______

Virginia City ______

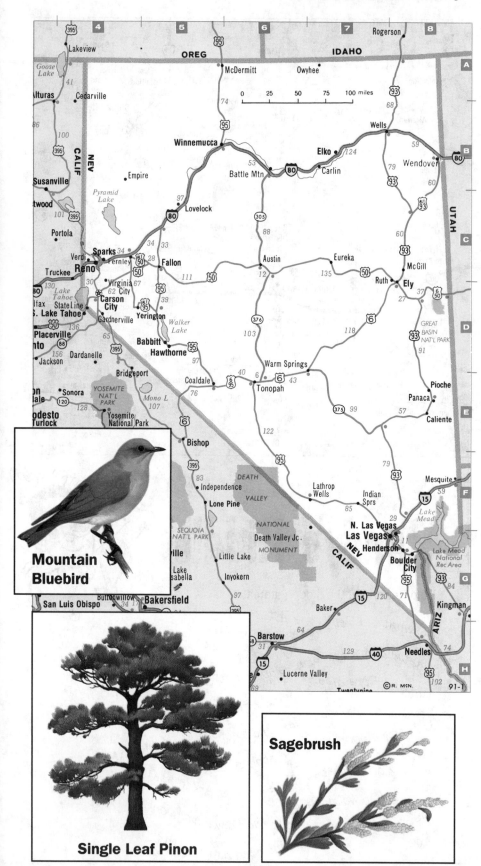

Mountain Bluebird

Single Leaf Pinon

Sagebrush

NEW HAMPSHIRE

Capital: Concord

Fantastic Forest

Randy has found a radical tree. See if you can tell where each leaf really belongs. Then color the leaves in autumn colors.

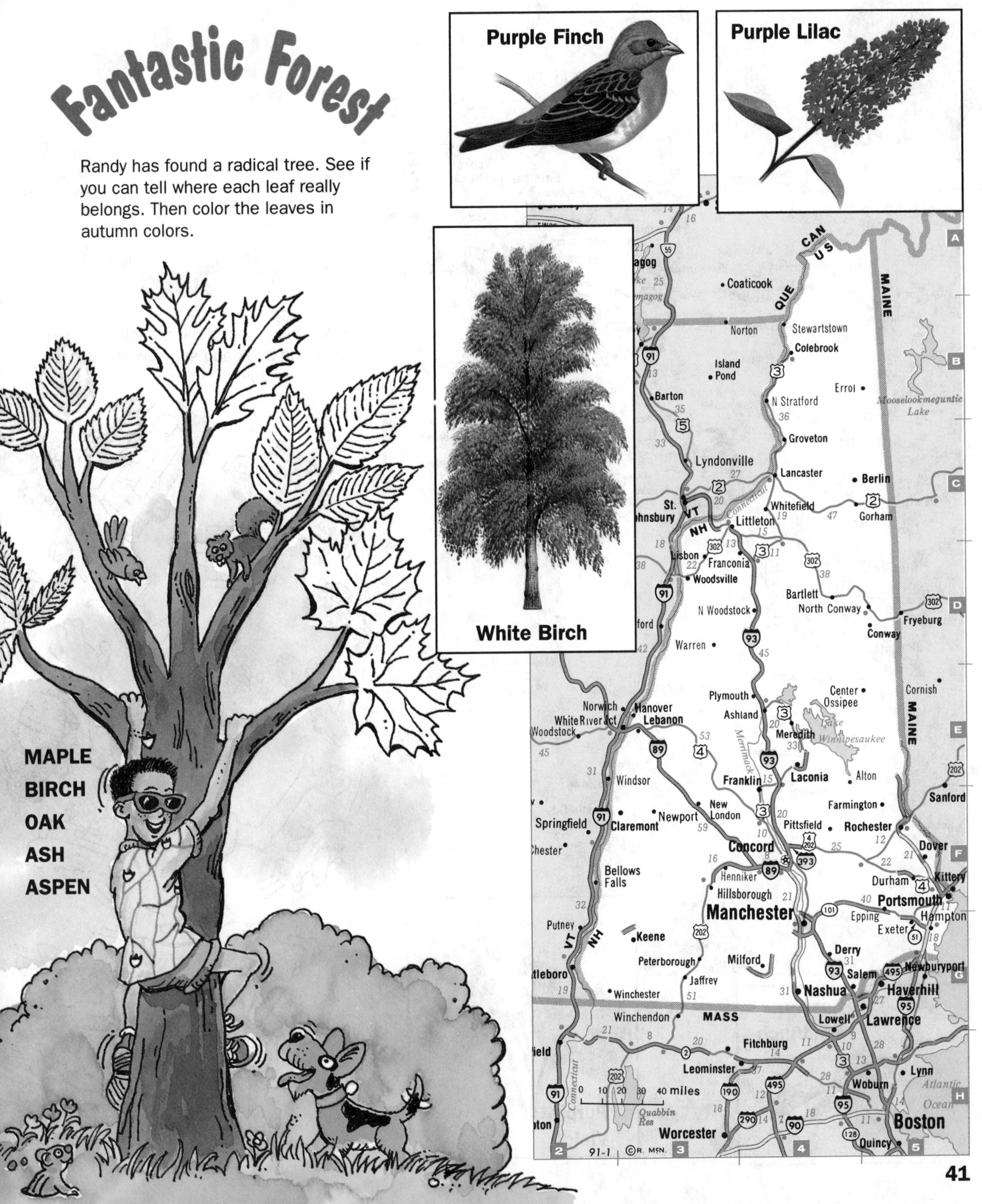

Red Oak

NEW JERSEY

Capital: Trenton

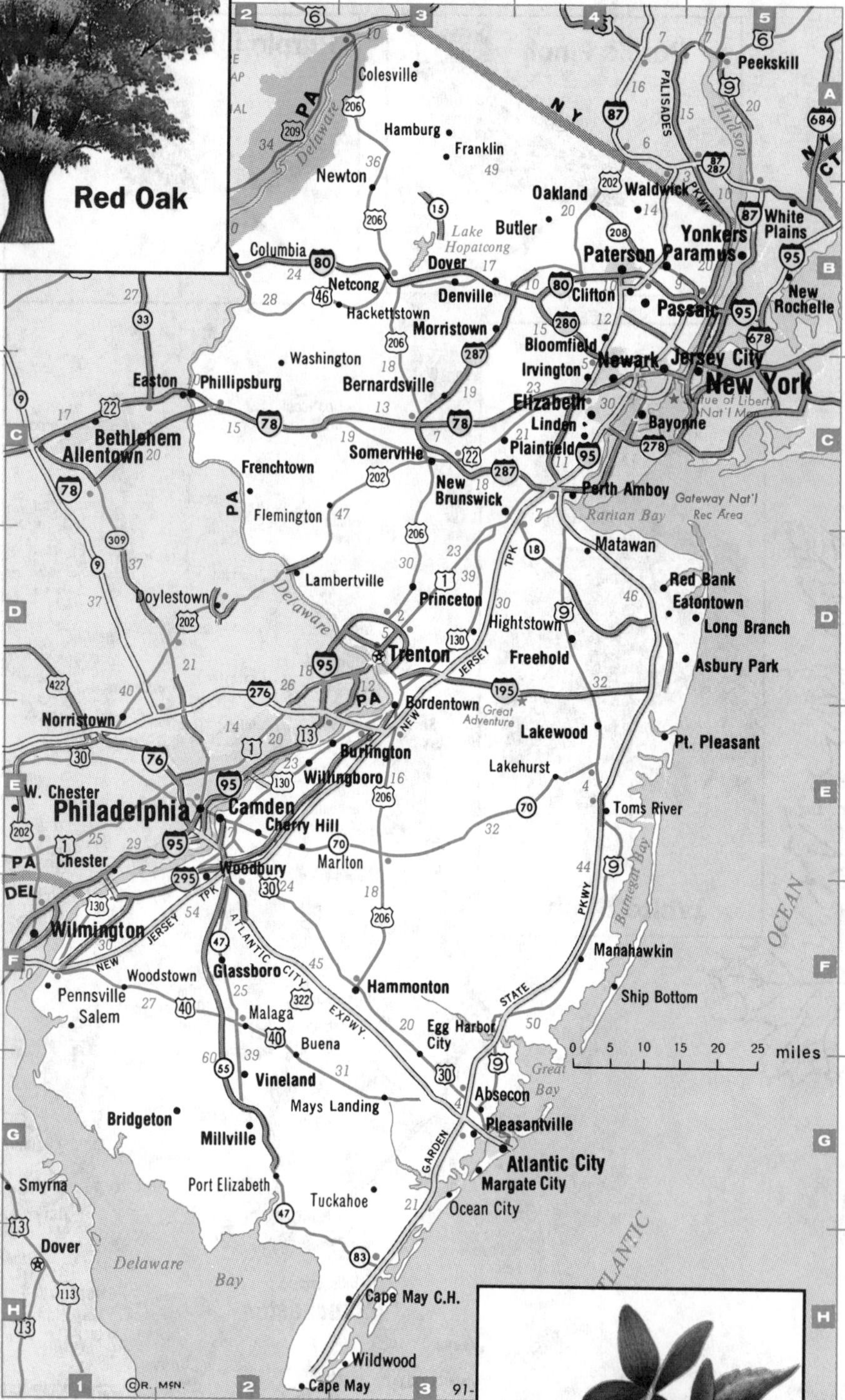

Eastern Goldfinch

Purple Violet

Study these things for one minute, then close the book and see how many you can remember.

NEW MEXICO

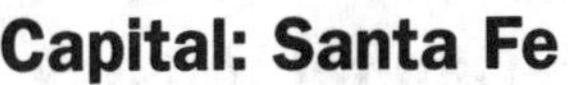

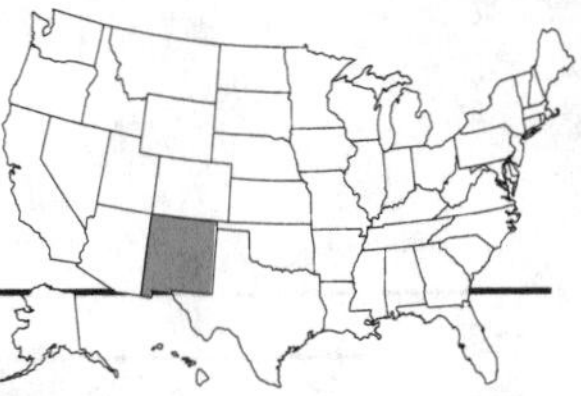

Capital: Santa Fe

Yucca

Pinon

Roadrunner

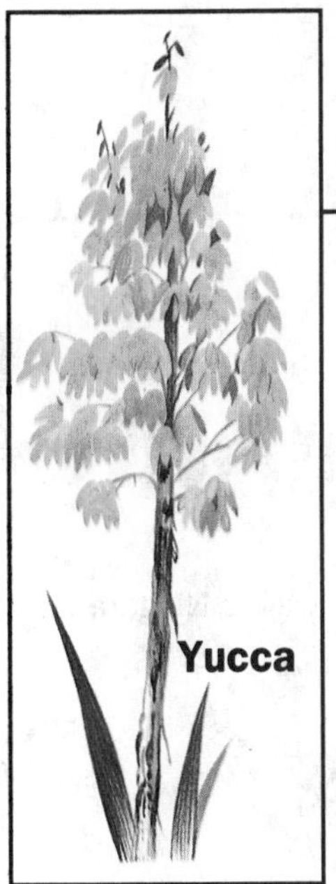

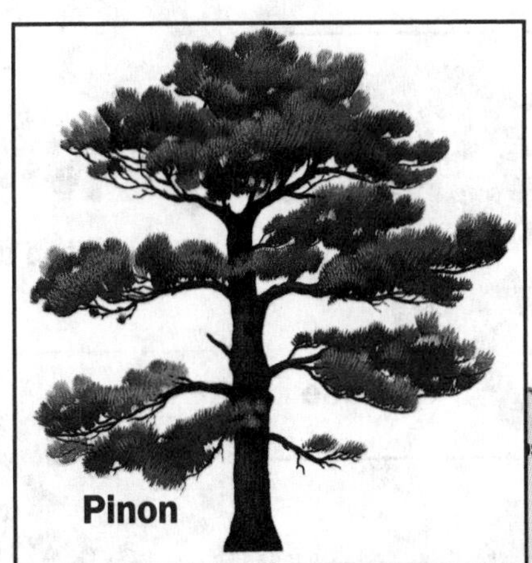

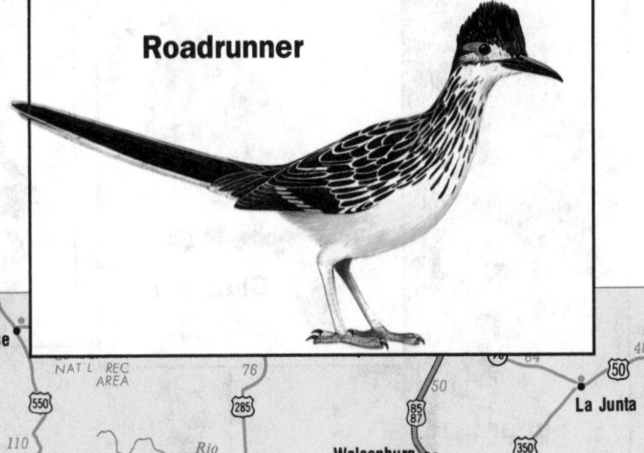

Up, Up and Away!

Connect the dots and color the picture in bright colors.

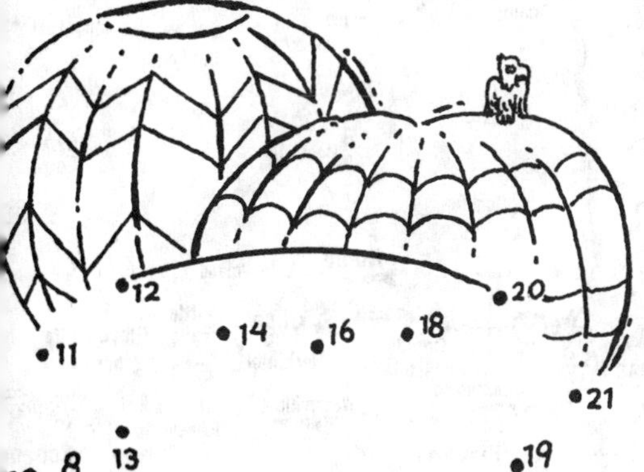

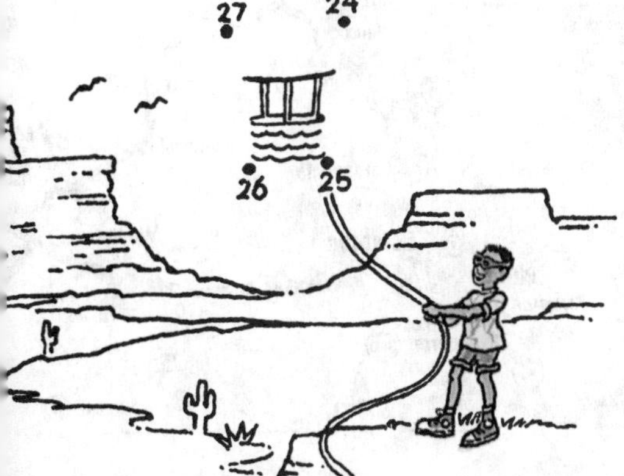

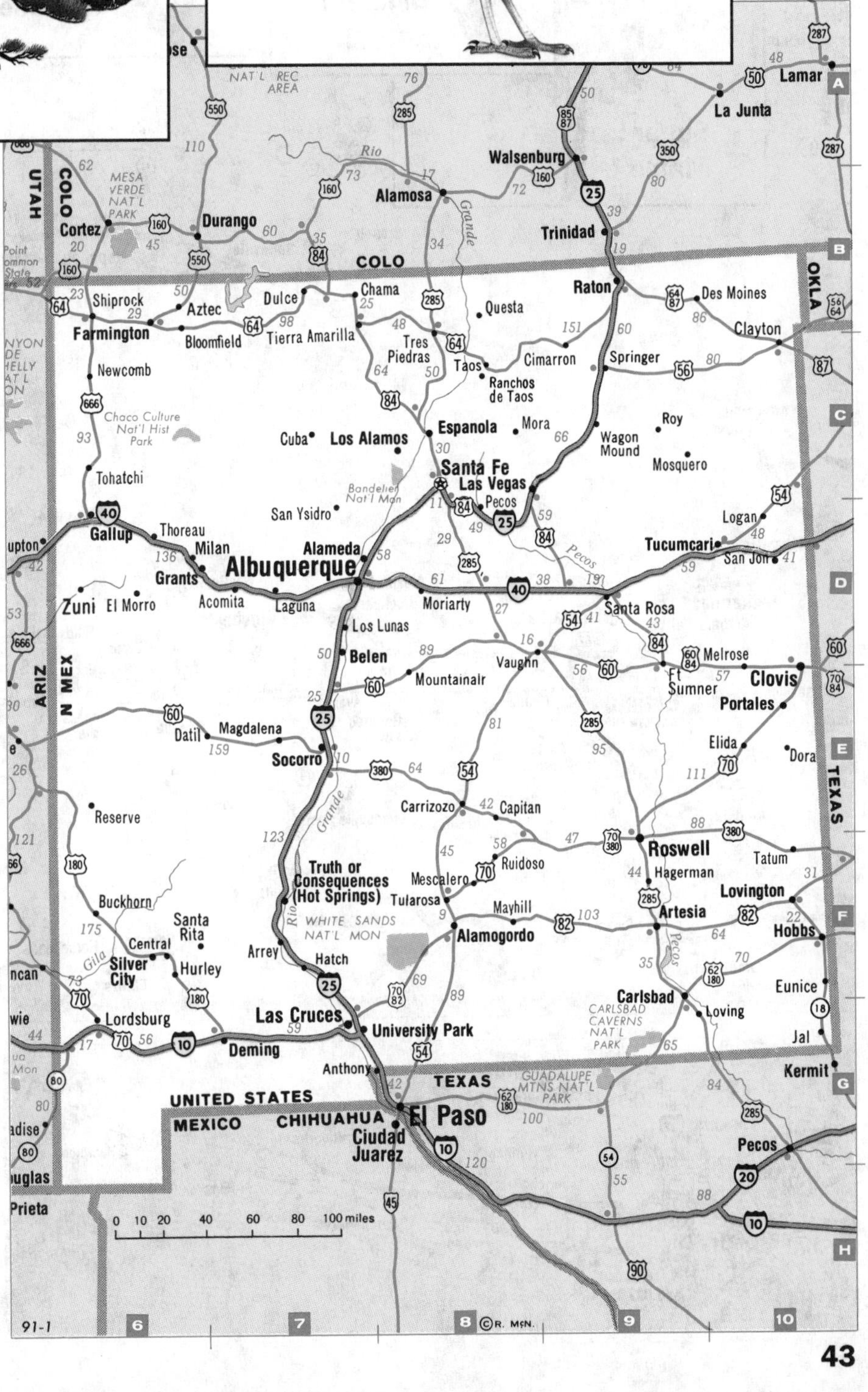

NEW YORK

Capital: Albany

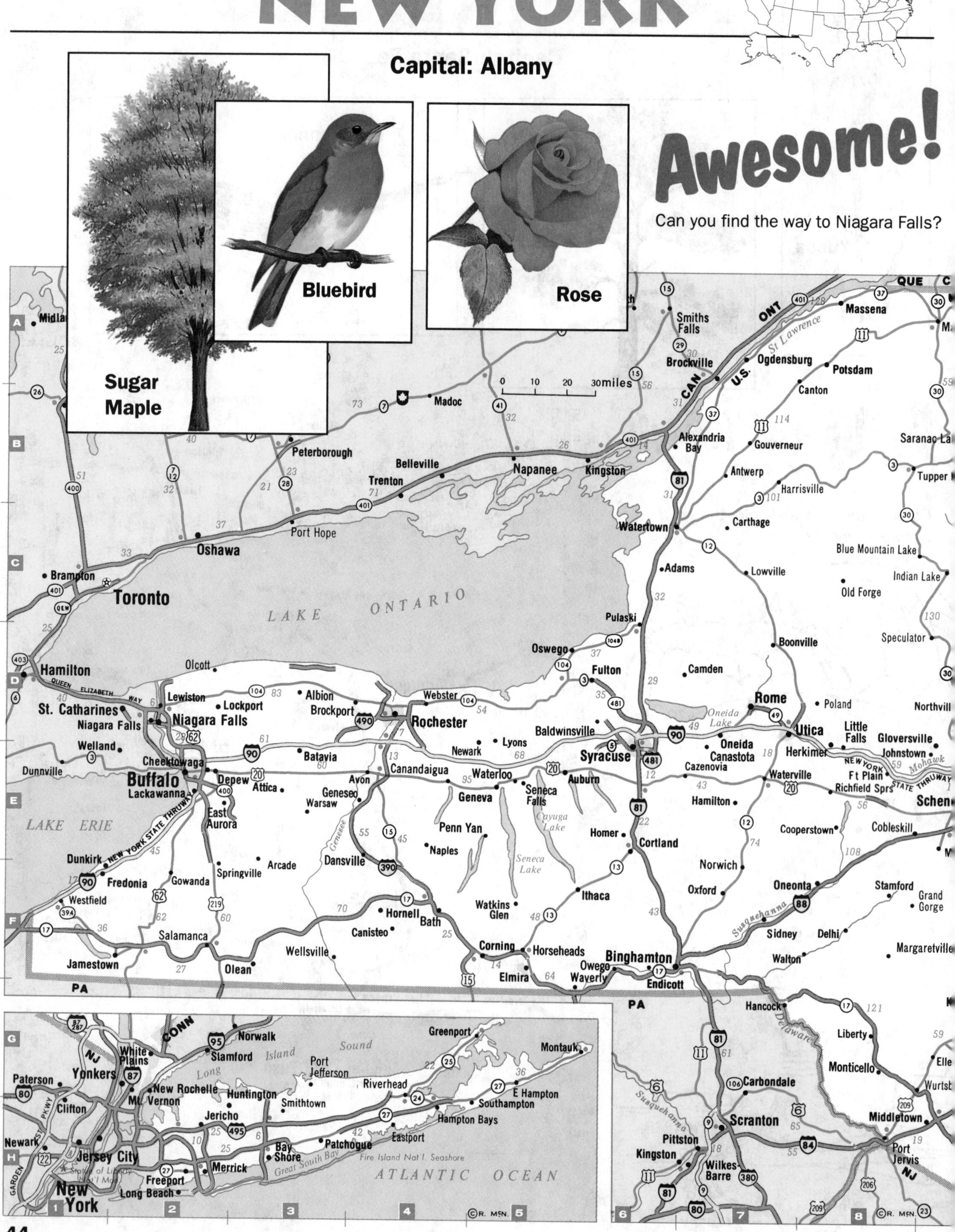

Awesome!

Can you find the way to Niagara Falls?

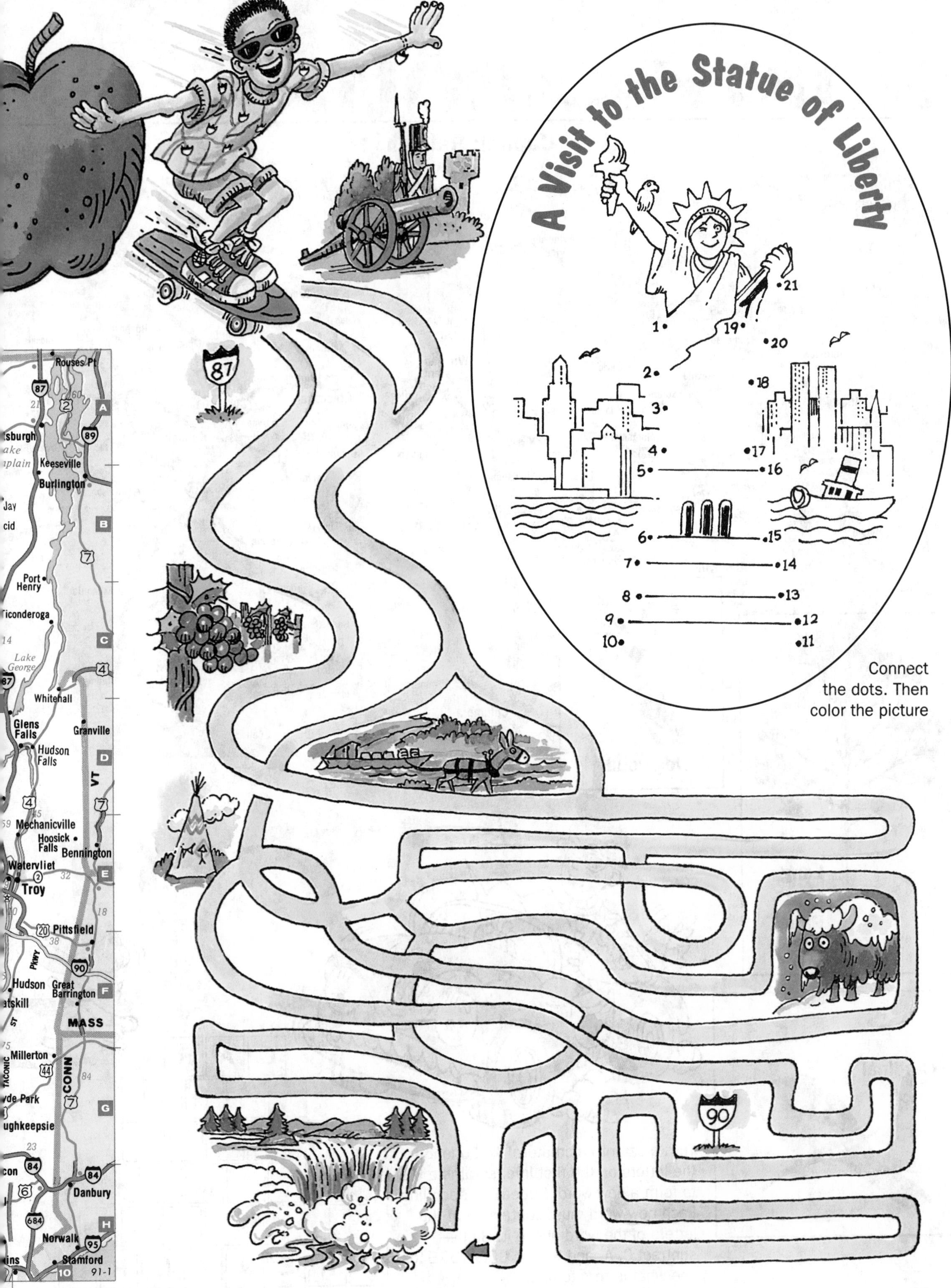
A Visit to the Statue of Liberty
1 2 3 4 5 6 7 8 9 10 11 12 13 14 15 16 17 18 19 20 21
Connect the dots. Then color the picture
87
90
Rouses Pt
Keeseville
Burlington
Port Henry
Ticonderoga
Lake George
Whitehall
Glens Falls
Granville
Hudson Falls
VT
Mechanicville
Hoosick Falls
Bennington
Watervliet
Troy
Pittsfield
Hudson
Great Barrington
MASS
Millerton
TACONIC
CONN
Poughkeepsie
Danbury
Norwalk
Stamford

NORTH CAROLINA

Capital: Raleigh

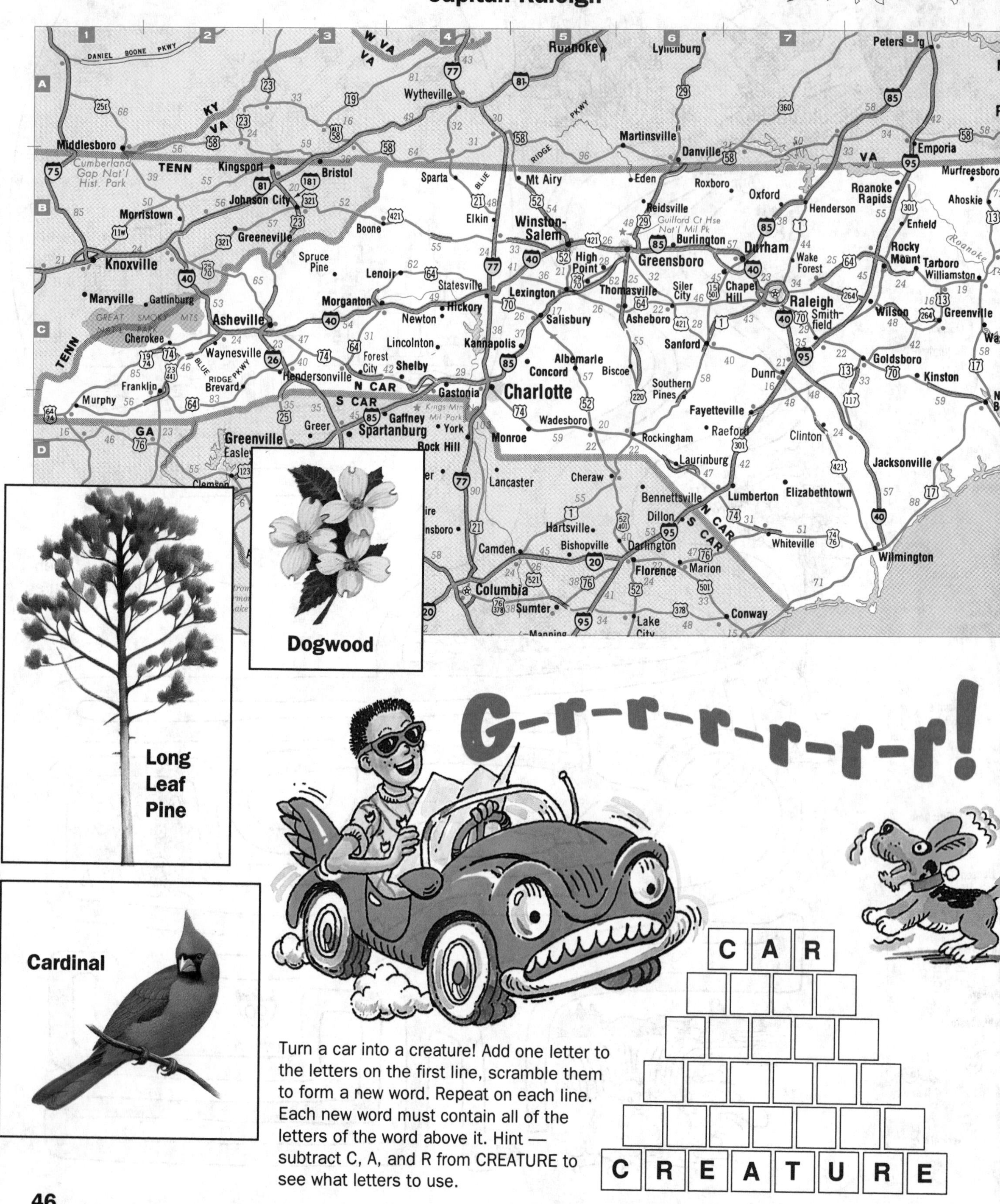

Turn a car into a creature! Add one letter to the letters on the first line, scramble them to form a new word. Repeat on each line. Each new word must contain all of the letters of the word above it. Hint — subtract C, A, and R from CREATURE to see what letters to use.

Safety First!

Can you identify each sign? Then put its number next to its description.

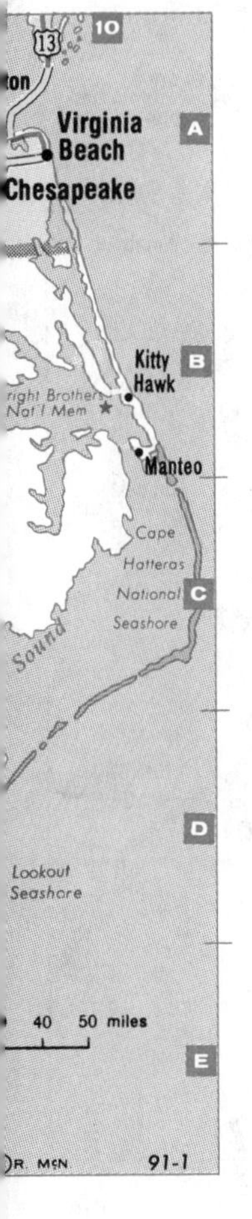

___ Merge
___ No Passing Zone
___ Do Not Enter
___ School Crossing
___ Slippery When Wet
___ Farm Machinery
___ No Right Turn
___ Cattle Crossing
___ Pedestrian Crossing
___ Stop
___ Road Curves
___ No U-Turn
___ Steep Hill
___ Yield
___ Deer Crossing
___ Railroad Crossing
___ Cross Road
___ No Bicycles

NORTH DAKOTA

Capital: Bismarck

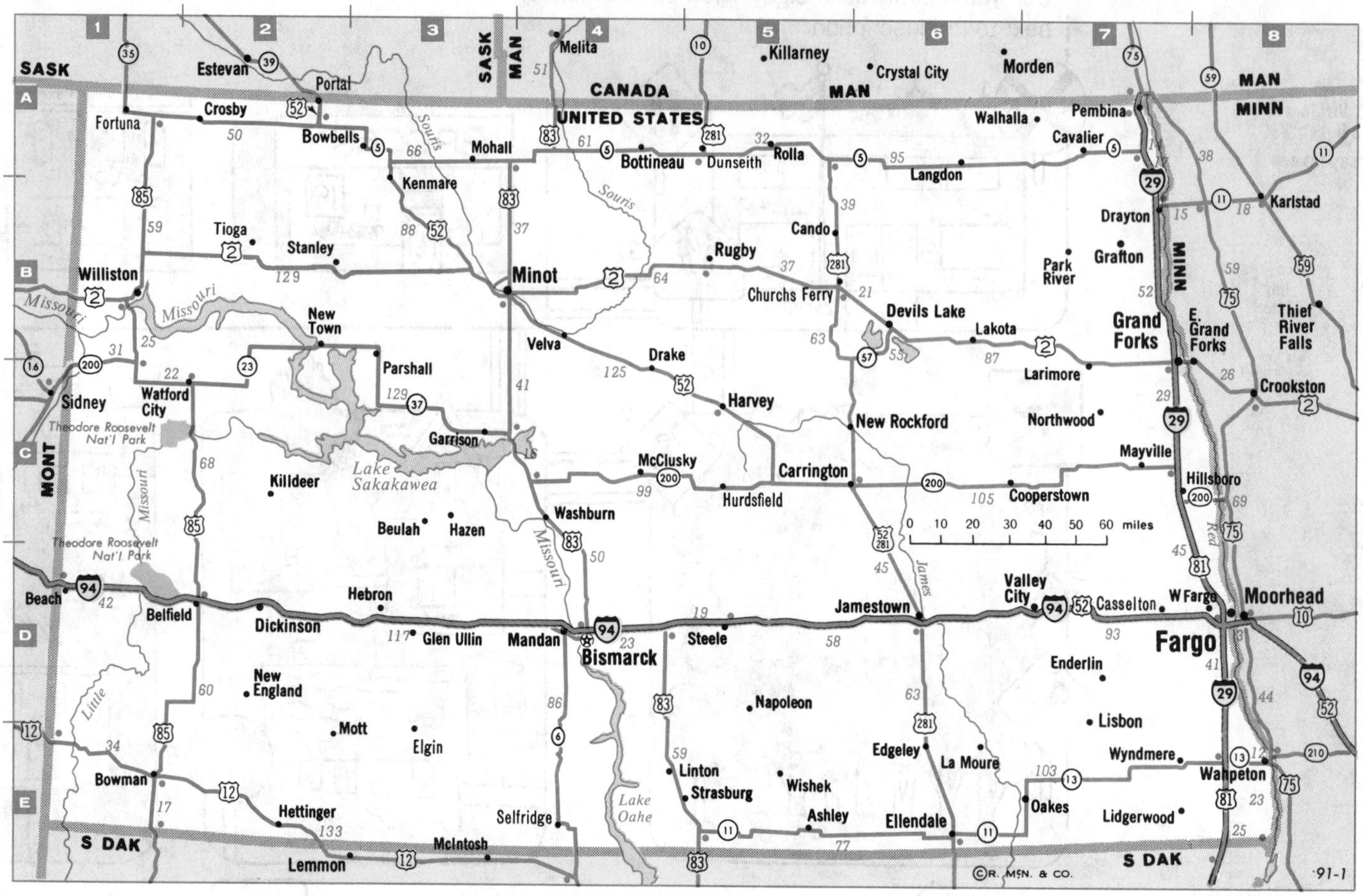

SASK
MAN
CANADA
UNITED STATES
MINN
MONT
S DAK
Estevan
Portal
Melita
Killarney
Crystal City
Morden
Fortuna
Crosby
Bowbells
Mohall
Bottineau
Dunseith
Rolla
Langdon
Walhalla
Pembina
Cavalier
Kenmare
Tioga
Stanley
Minot
Rugby
Cando
Churchs Ferry
Drayton
Grafton
Park River
Karlstad
Williston
New Town
Parshall
Velva
Drake
Devils Lake
Lakota
Grand Forks
E. Grand Forks
Thief River Falls
Sidney
Watford City
Theodore Roosevelt Nat'l Park
Garrison
Lake Sakakawea
Harvey
New Rockford
Larimore
Northwood
Crookston
Killdeer
McClusky
Carrington
Hurdsfield
Mayville
Cooperstown
Hillsboro
Beulah
Hazen
Washburn
Missouri
Souris
James
Red
Little
0 10 20 30 40 50 60 miles
Beach
Belfield
Dickinson
Hebron
Glen Ullin
Mandan
Bismarck
Steele
Jamestown
Valley City
Casselton
W Fargo
Fargo
Moorhead
New England
Napoleon
Enderlin
Lisbon
Mott
Elgin
Edgeley
La Moure
Wyndmere
Wahpeton
Bowman
Linton
Strasburg
Wishek
Lake Oahe
Hettinger
Selfridge
Ashley
Ellendale
Oakes
Lidgerwood
Lemmon
McIntosh
©R. McN. & CO.
91-1

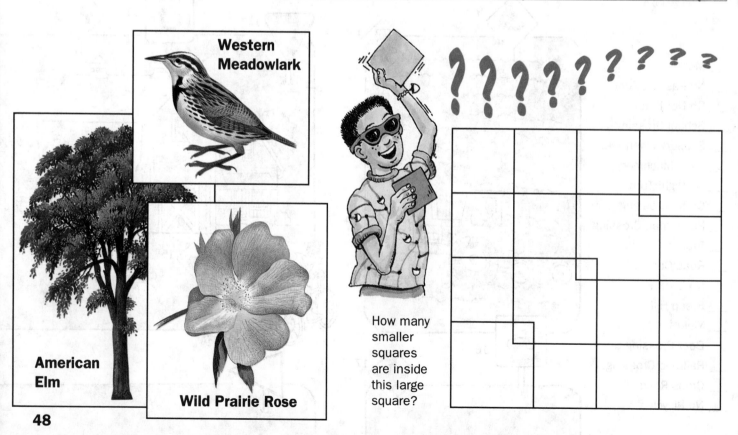

Western Meadowlark

American Elm

Wild Prairie Rose

How many smaller squares are inside this large square?

OKLAHOMA

Capital: Oklahoma City

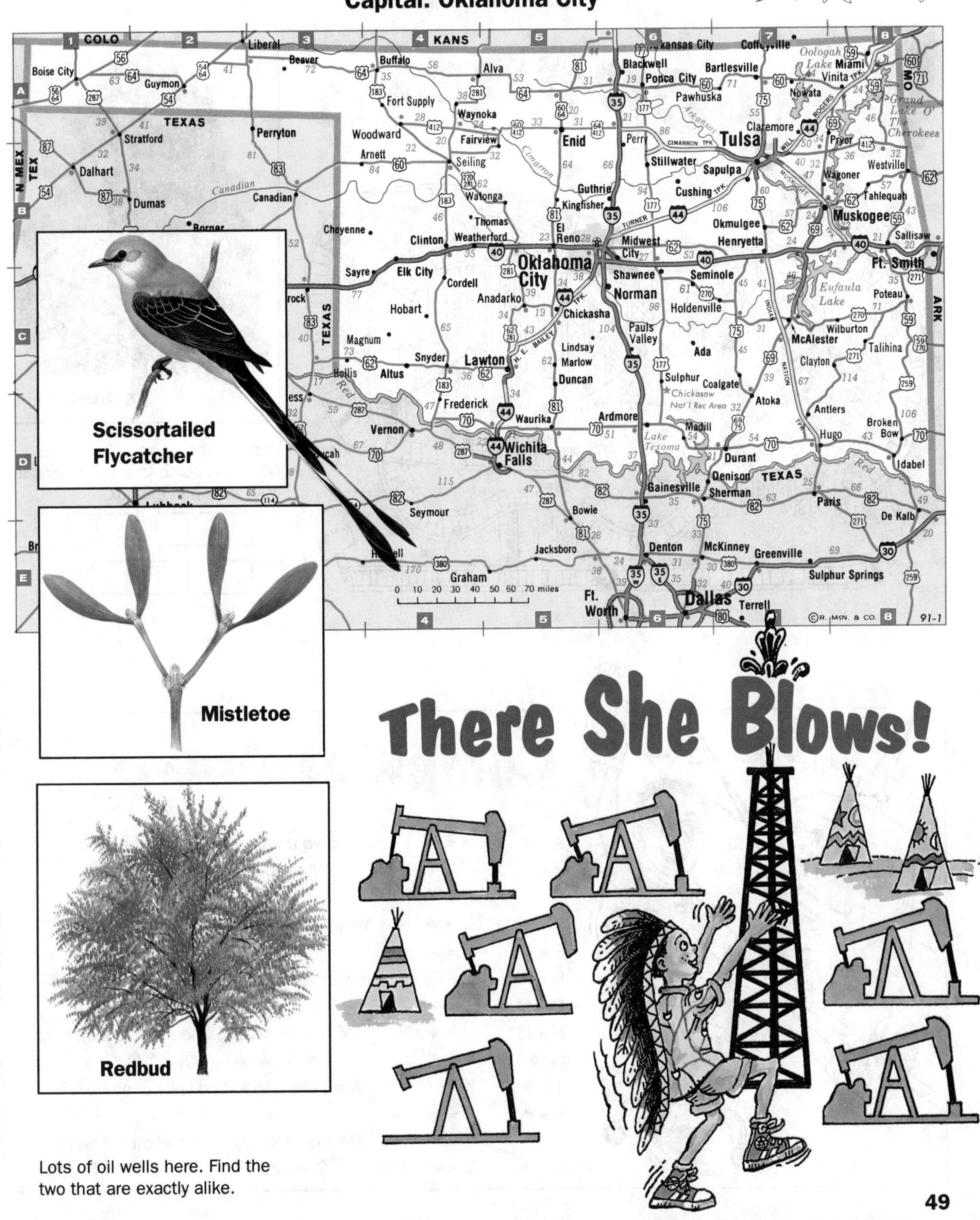

Scissortailed Flycatcher

Mistletoe

Redbud

There She Blows!

Lots of oil wells here. Find the two that are exactly alike.

OHIO

Capital: Columbus

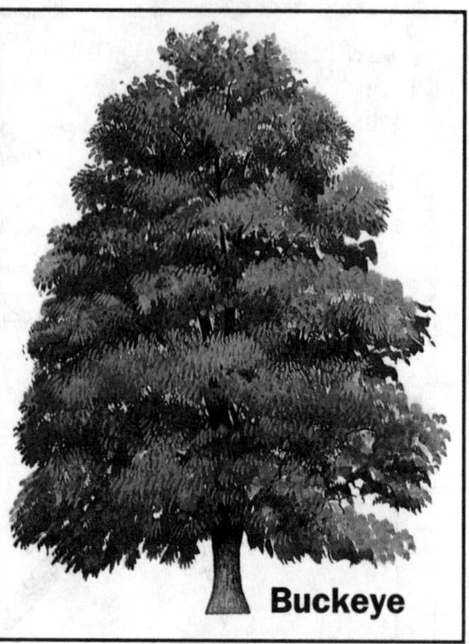
Buckeye

Catch a ride on an Ohio coaster. When you come to a letter along the way, write it in the box.

Computer Crazy!

A = ◆	N = Θ
B = ✳	O = ↑
C = √	P = ▼
D = △	Q = Φ
E = ◇	R = ☆
F = ✕	S = □
G = ■	T = ▲
H = ∅	U = ↓
I = ✹	V = ⊙
J = ●	W = ¥
K = ✚	X = ∸
L = ▽	Y = →
M = #	Z = ←

Solve these riddles with the code

What speaks every language?
◆Θ ◇√∅↑

Why shouldn't you tell secrets to a bean?
✳◇◆Θ□ ▲◆▽✚

What never leaves, but is always going out?
◆ √◆Θ△▽◇

What runs around when you tie it up?
→↑↓☆ □∅↑◇

What has a head and tail, but no body?
◆ √↑✹Θ

What coat is only put on when it is wet?
◆ √↑◆▲ ↑✕ ▼◆✹Θ▲

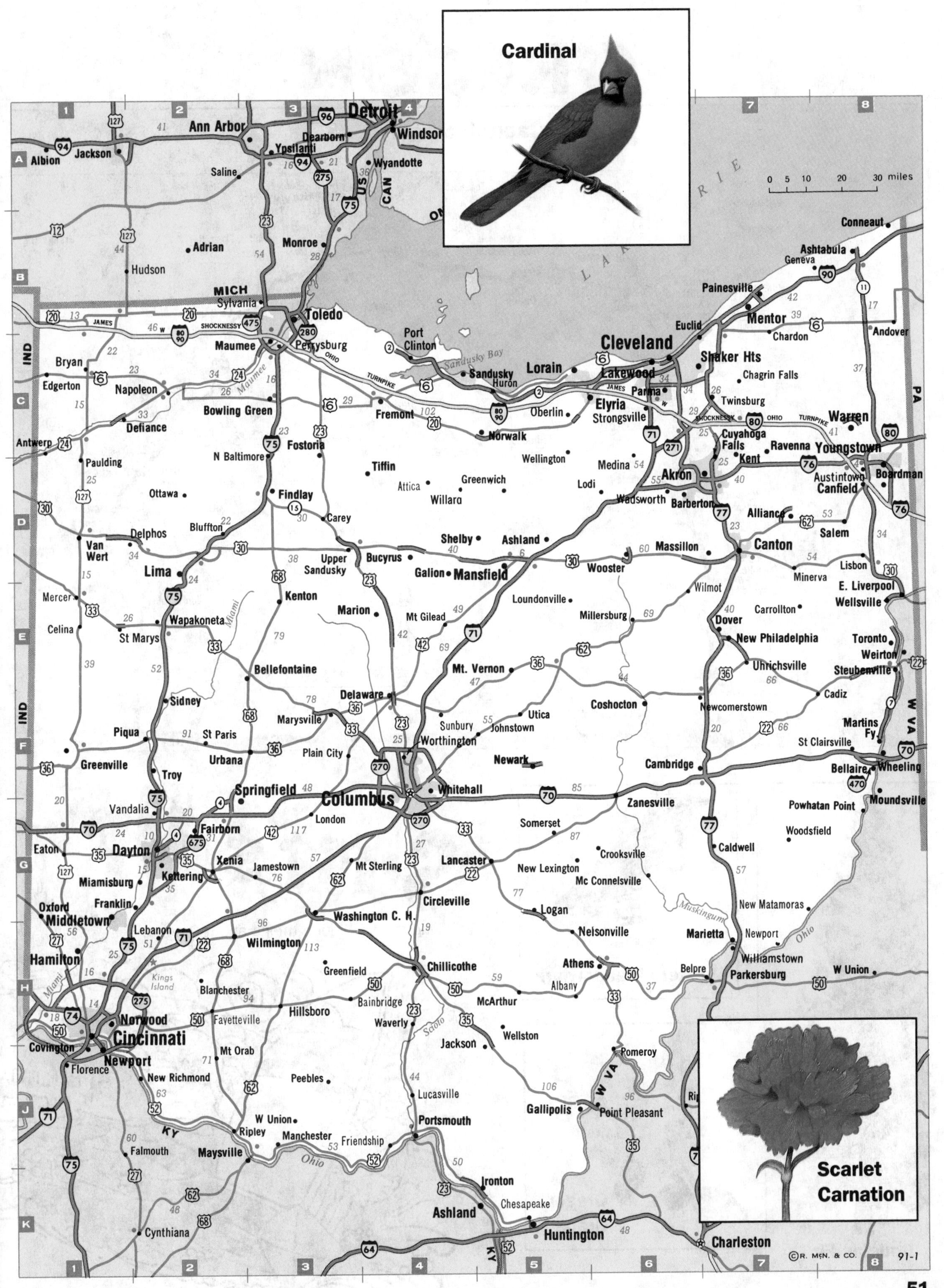

Cardinal
Scarlet Carnation
0 5 10 20 30 miles
LAKE ERIE
MICH
IND
PA
W VA
KY
CAN
Detroit
Windsor
Ann Arbor
Dearborn
Ypsilanti
Wyandotte
Albion
Jackson
Saline
Adrian
Hudson
Monroe
Sylvania
Toledo
Maumee
Perrysburg
Port Clinton
Sandusky Bay
Sandusky
Huron
Lorain
Cleveland
Lakewood
Euclid
Painesville
Mentor
Chardon
Geneva
Ashtabula
Conneaut
Andover
Shaker Hts
Chagrin Falls
Parma
Twinsburg
Elyria
Oberlin
Strongsville
Warren
Youngstown
Cuyahoga Falls
Kent
Ravenna
Akron
Boardman
Austintown
Canfield
Medina
Wellington
Lodi
Wadsworth
Barberton
Alliance
Salem
Canton
Massillon
Wooster
Lisbon
Minerva
E. Liverpool
Wellsville
Carrollton
Wilmot
Dover
New Philadelphia
Toronto
Weirton
Steubenville
Uhrichsville
Cadiz
Newcomerstown
Coshocton
Martins Fy
St Clairsville
Bellaire
Wheeling
Moundsville
Powhatan Point
Woodsfield
Cambridge
Zanesville
Caldwell
Crooksville
Mc Connelsville
New Lexington
Somerset
New Matamoras
Marietta
Newport
Williamstown
Parkersburg
Belpre
W Union
Athens
Albany
Nelsonville
Logan
Lancaster
Bryan
Edgerton
Napoleon
Bowling Green
Defiance
Fremont
Norwalk
Antwerp
Paulding
N Baltimore
Fostoria
Tiffin
Attica
Greenwich
Willard
Ottawa
Findlay
Carey
Bluffton
Delphos
Van Wert
Lima
Upper Sandusky
Bucyrus
Shelby
Ashland
Galion
Mansfield
Loundonville
Millersburg
Kenton
Marion
Mt Gilead
Mercer
Celina
Wapakoneta
St Marys
Bellefontaine
Mt. Vernon
Delaware
Sidney
Marysville
Sunbury
Utica
Johnstown
Worthington
Newark
Piqua
St Paris
Urbana
Plain City
Greenville
Troy
Springfield
Columbus
Whitehall
Vandalia
Fairborn
London
Eaton
Dayton
Xenia
Jamestown
Kettering
Miamisburg
Mt Sterling
Circleville
Franklin
Oxford
Middletown
Lebanon
Washington C. H.
Wilmington
Hamilton
Kings Island
Greenfield
Chillicothe
Blanchester
Bainbridge
McArthur
Hillsboro
Norwood
Cincinnati
Fayetteville
Waverly
Wellston
Covington
Newport
Florence
Mt Orab
Jackson
Pomeroy
New Richmond
Peebles
Lucasville
Gallipolis
Point Pleasant
W Union
Ripley
Manchester
Friendship
Portsmouth
Falmouth
Maysville
Ironton
Ashland
Chesapeake
Cynthiana
Huntington
Charleston
Miami
Maumee
Scioto
Muskingum
Ohio
OHIO TURNPIKE
JAMES SHOCKNESSY
©R. McN. & CO.
91-1

OREGON

Capital: Salem

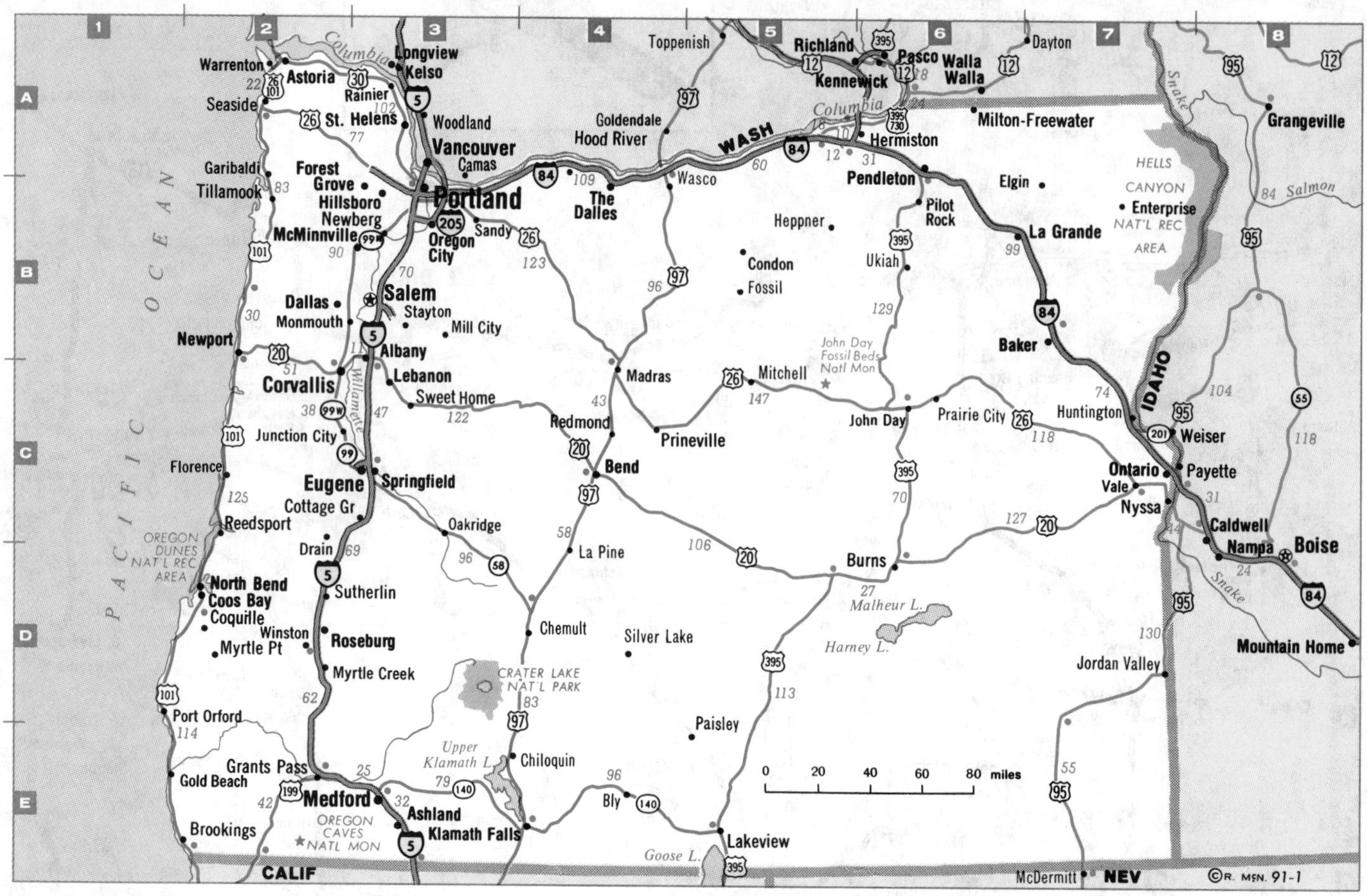

Douglas Fir

Western Meadowlark

Oregon Grape

Surf's Up!

Find the six hidden things about Oregon.

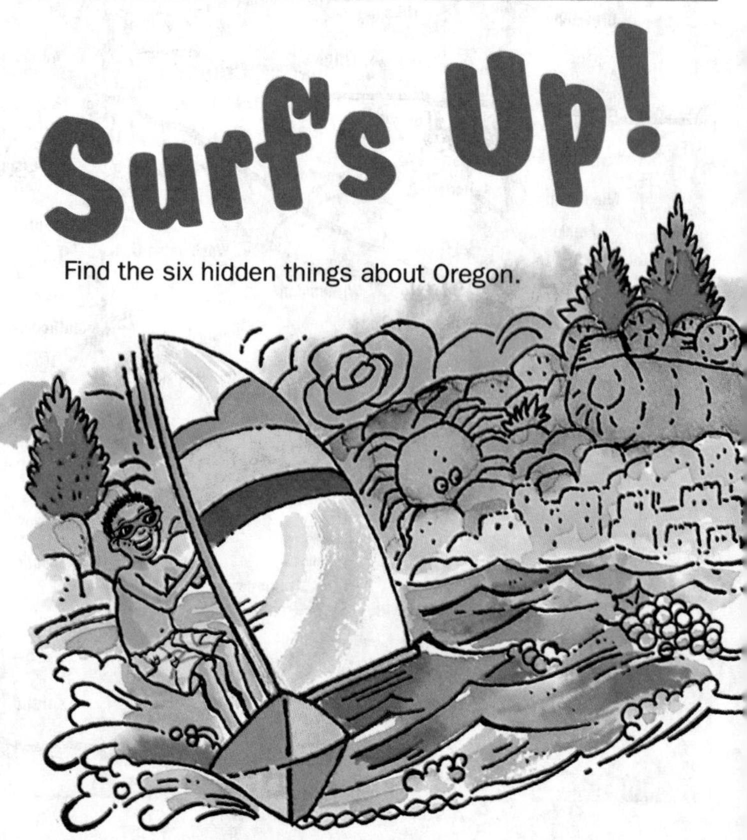

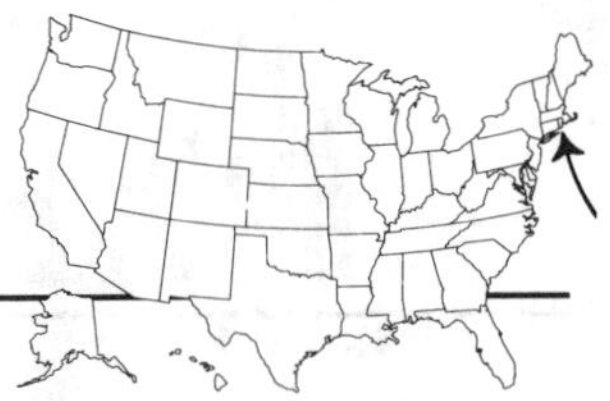

RHODE ISLAND

Capital: Providence

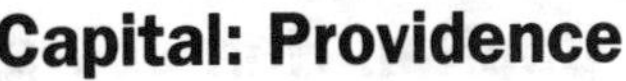

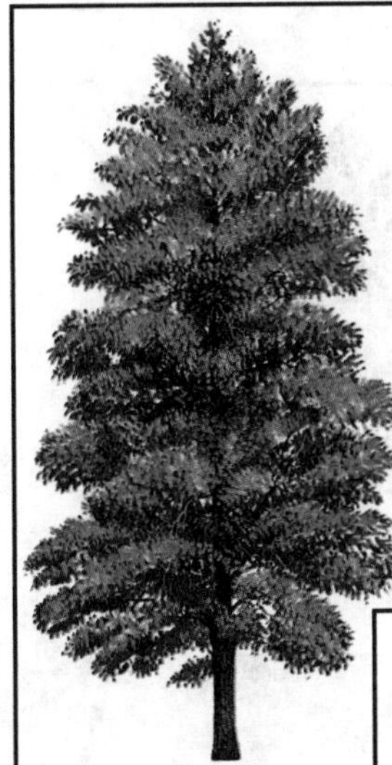

Red Maple

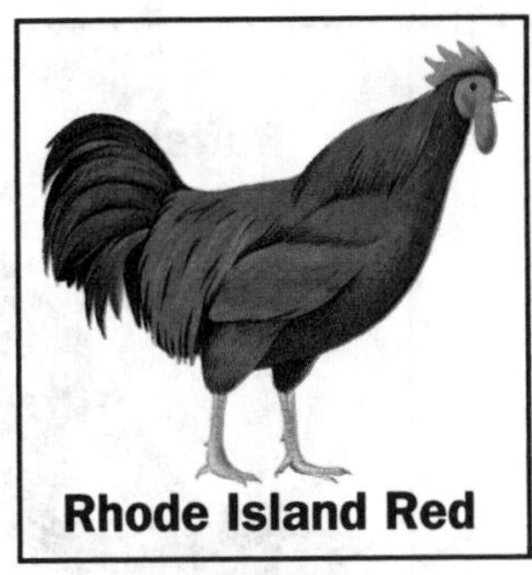

Rhode Island Red

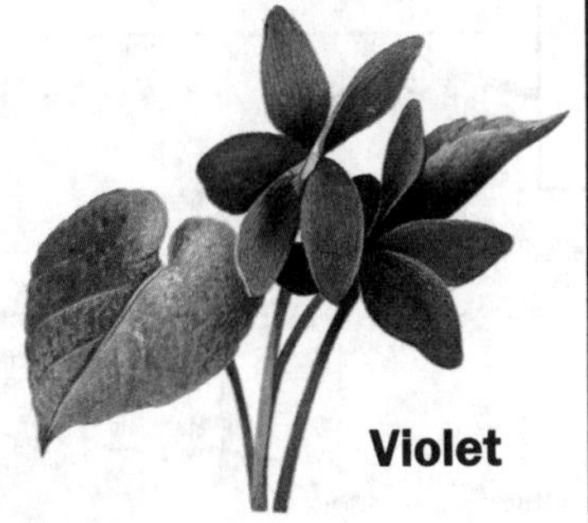

Violet

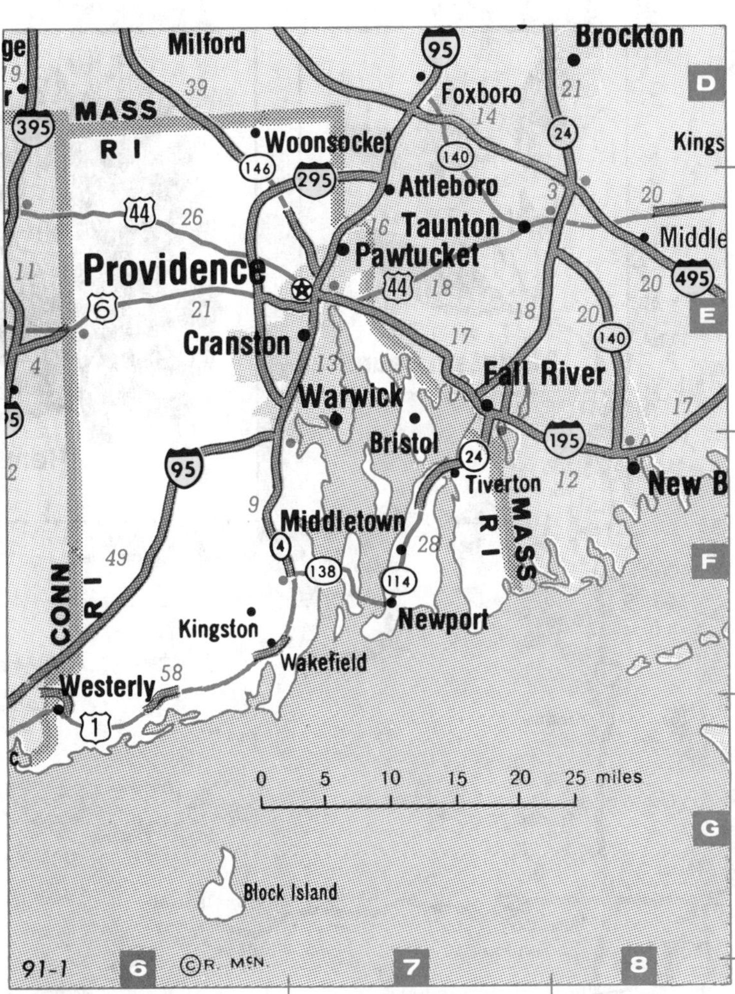

Mother Hen has lost her chicks. Help Randy find them for her.

Cluck! Cluck!

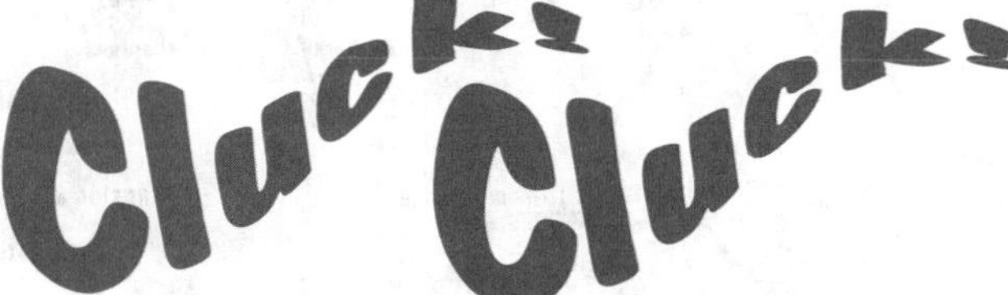

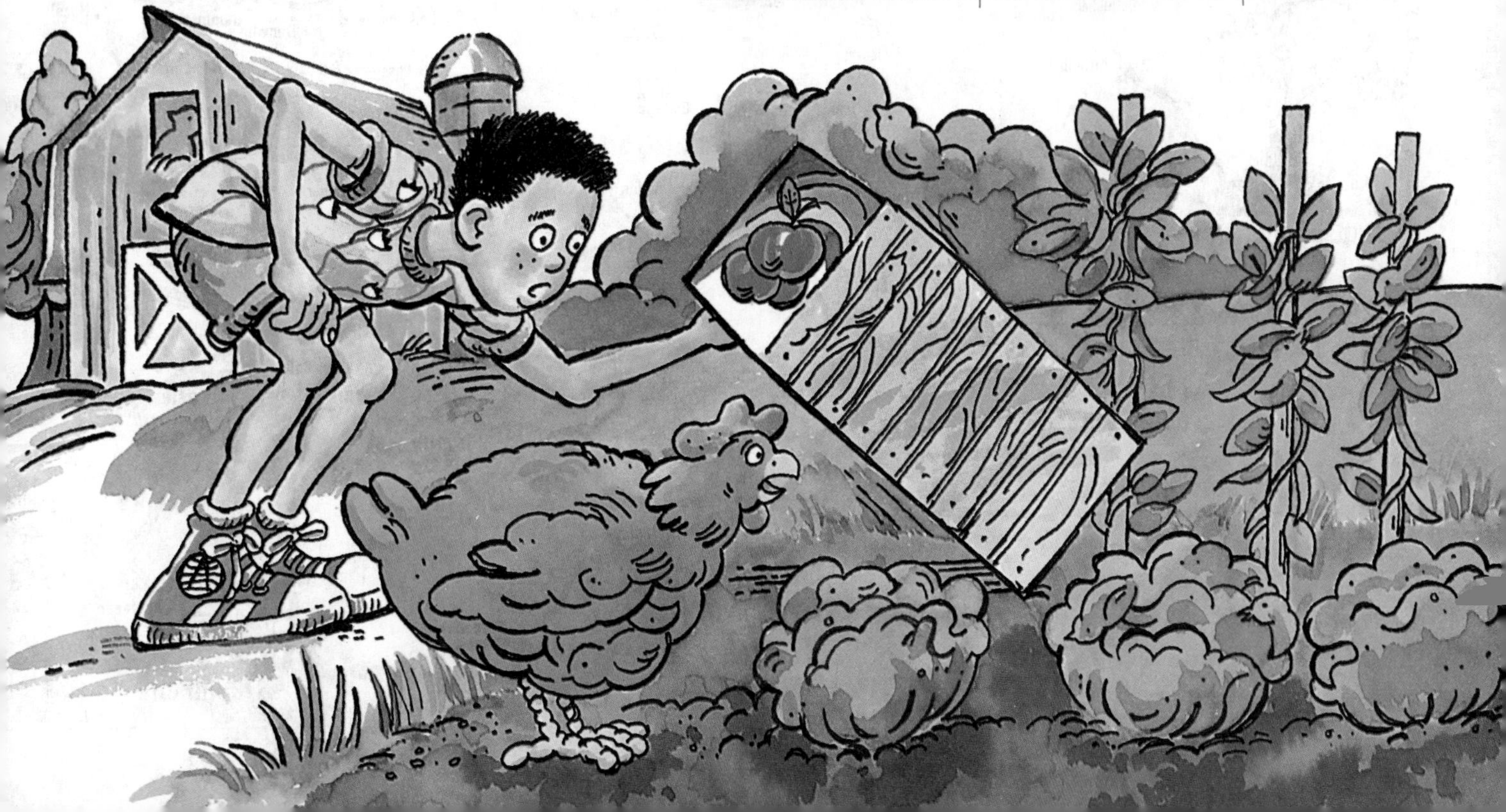

PENNSYLVANIA

Capital: Harrisburg

Mountain Laurel

Hemlock

Ruffed Grouse

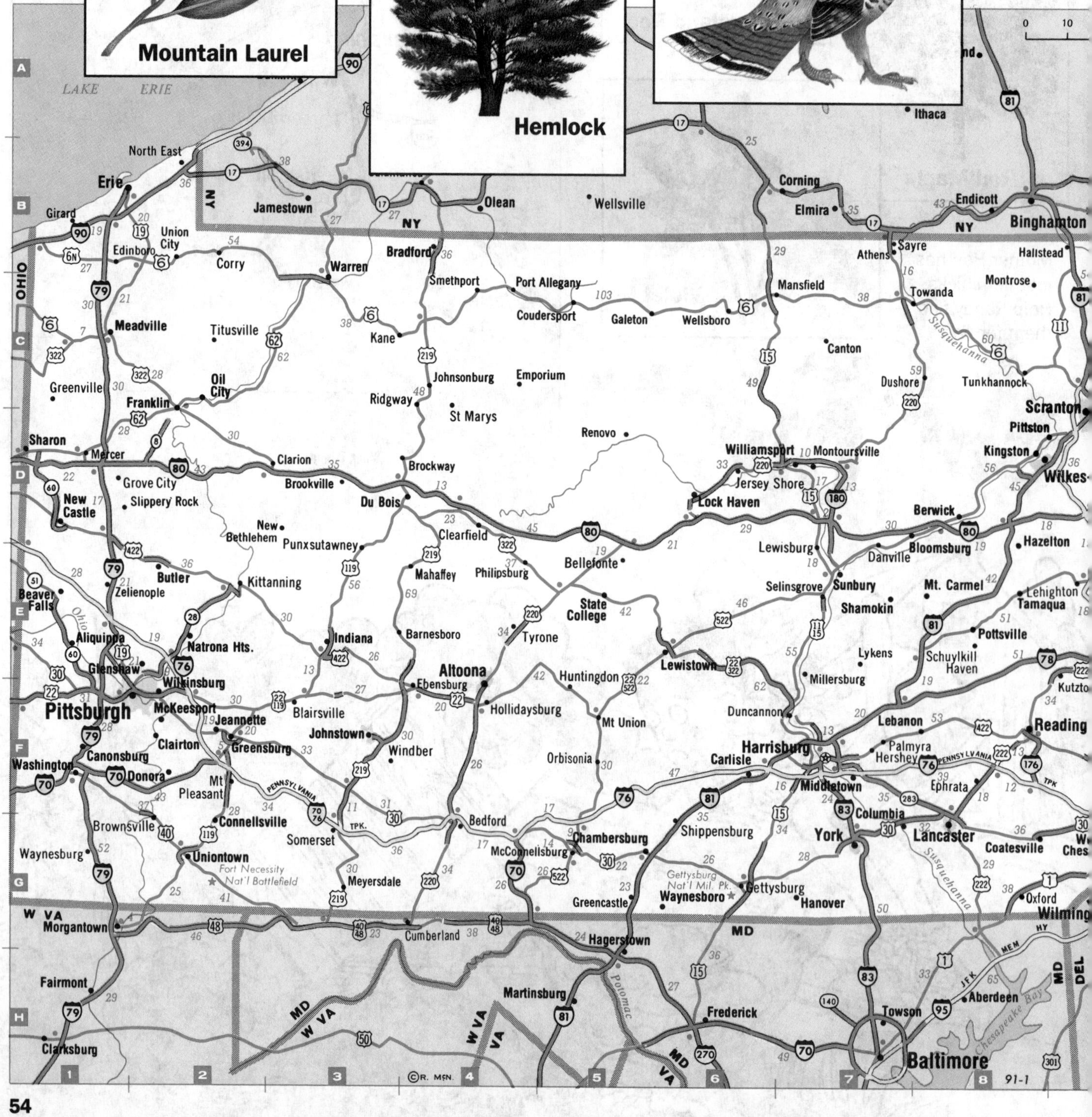

LAKE ERIE

North East
Erie
Girard
Edinboro
Union City
Corry
Jamestown
Warren
Olean
Wellsville
Bradford
Smethport
Port Allegany
Coudersport
Galeton
Wellsboro
Mansfield
Corning
Elmira
Ithaca
Endicott
Binghamton
Athens
Sayre
Towanda
Montrose
Hallstead
Meadville
Titusville
Kane
Canton
Dushore
Tunkhannock
Scranton
Pittston
Kingston
Wilkes-
Greenville
Oil City
Franklin
Johnsonburg
Emporium
Ridgway
St Marys
Renovo
Sharon
Mercer
Clarion
Brockway
Williamsport
Montoursville
Jersey Shore
Lock Haven
Grove City
Brookville
Du Bois
New Castle
Slippery Rock
New Bethlehem
Punxsutawney
Clearfield
Berwick
Lewisburg
Bloomsburg
Danville
Hazelton
Butler
Kittanning
Mahaffey
Philipsburg
Bellefonte
Beaver Falls
Zelienople
Selinsgrove
Sunbury
Shamokin
Mt. Carmel
Lehighton
Tamaqua
State College
Tyrone
Aliquippa
Natrona Hts.
Indiana
Barnesboro
Pottsville
Lykens
Schuylkill Haven
Glenshaw
Wilkinsburg
Altoona
Ebensburg
Huntingdon
Lewistown
Millersburg
Pittsburgh
McKeesport
Jeannette
Blairsville
Hollidaysburg
Mt Union
Duncannon
Lebanon
Reading
Kutztown
Clairton
Greensburg
Johnstown
Windber
Harrisburg
Palmyra
Hershey
Washington
Canonsburg
Donora
Mt Pleasant
Orbisonia
Carlisle
Middletown
Ephrata
Brownsville
Connellsville
Somerset
Bedford
Chambersburg
Shippensburg
York
Columbia
Lancaster
Coatesville
Waynesburg
Uniontown
McConnellsburg
Fort Necessity Nat'l Battlefield
Meyersdale
Gettysburg Nat'l Mil. Pk.
Waynesboro
Gettysburg
Hanover
Greencastle
Oxford
Morgantown
Cumberland
Hagerstown
Fairmont
Martinsburg
Frederick
Towson
Aberdeen
Clarksburg
Baltimore
Chesapeake Bay
Susquehanna
Potomac
Ohio
OHIO
NY
W VA
MD
VA
DEL
PENNSYLVANIA TPK.

©R. McN.
91-1

What to do Where!

There's lots to see in Pennsylvania. Check out the city where you'll see each of these things. Fill in the number next to its city.

Gettysburg ________
Lancaster ________
Philadelphia ________
Pittsburgh ________
Punxsutawney ________
Scranton ________
Titusville ________
Williamsport ________

HOME OF LITTLE LEAGUE BASEBALL

1 2 3 4 5 6 7 8

ROOT BEER 1866

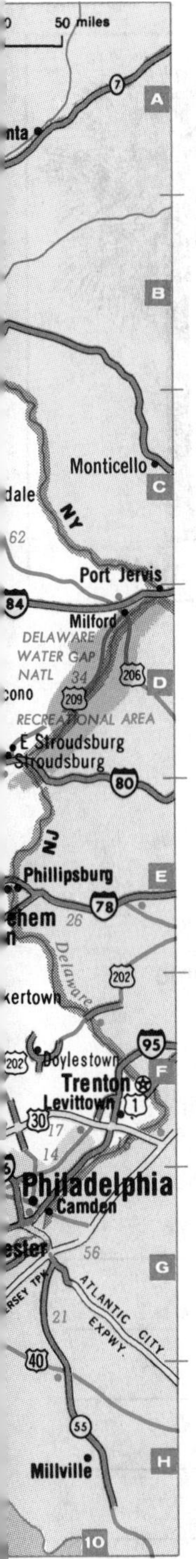

Trivia Time!

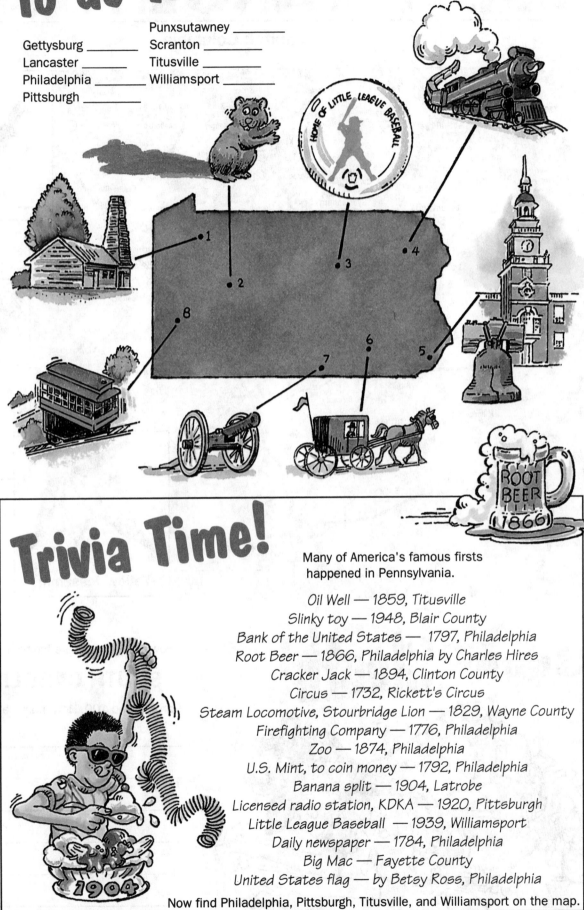

Many of America's famous firsts happened in Pennsylvania.

Oil Well — 1859, Titusville
Slinky toy — 1948, Blair County
Bank of the United States — 1797, Philadelphia
Root Beer — 1866, Philadelphia by Charles Hires
Cracker Jack — 1894, Clinton County
Circus — 1732, Rickett's Circus
Steam Locomotive, Stourbridge Lion — 1829, Wayne County
Firefighting Company — 1776, Philadelphia
Zoo — 1874, Philadelphia
U.S. Mint, to coin money — 1792, Philadelphia
Banana split — 1904, Latrobe
Licensed radio station, KDKA — 1920, Pittsburgh
Little League Baseball — 1939, Williamsport
Daily newspaper — 1784, Philadelphia
Big Mac — Fayette County
United States flag — by Betsy Ross, Philadelphia

1904

Now find Philadelphia, Pittsburgh, Titusville, and Williamsport on the map.

SOUTH CAROLINA

Capital: Columbia

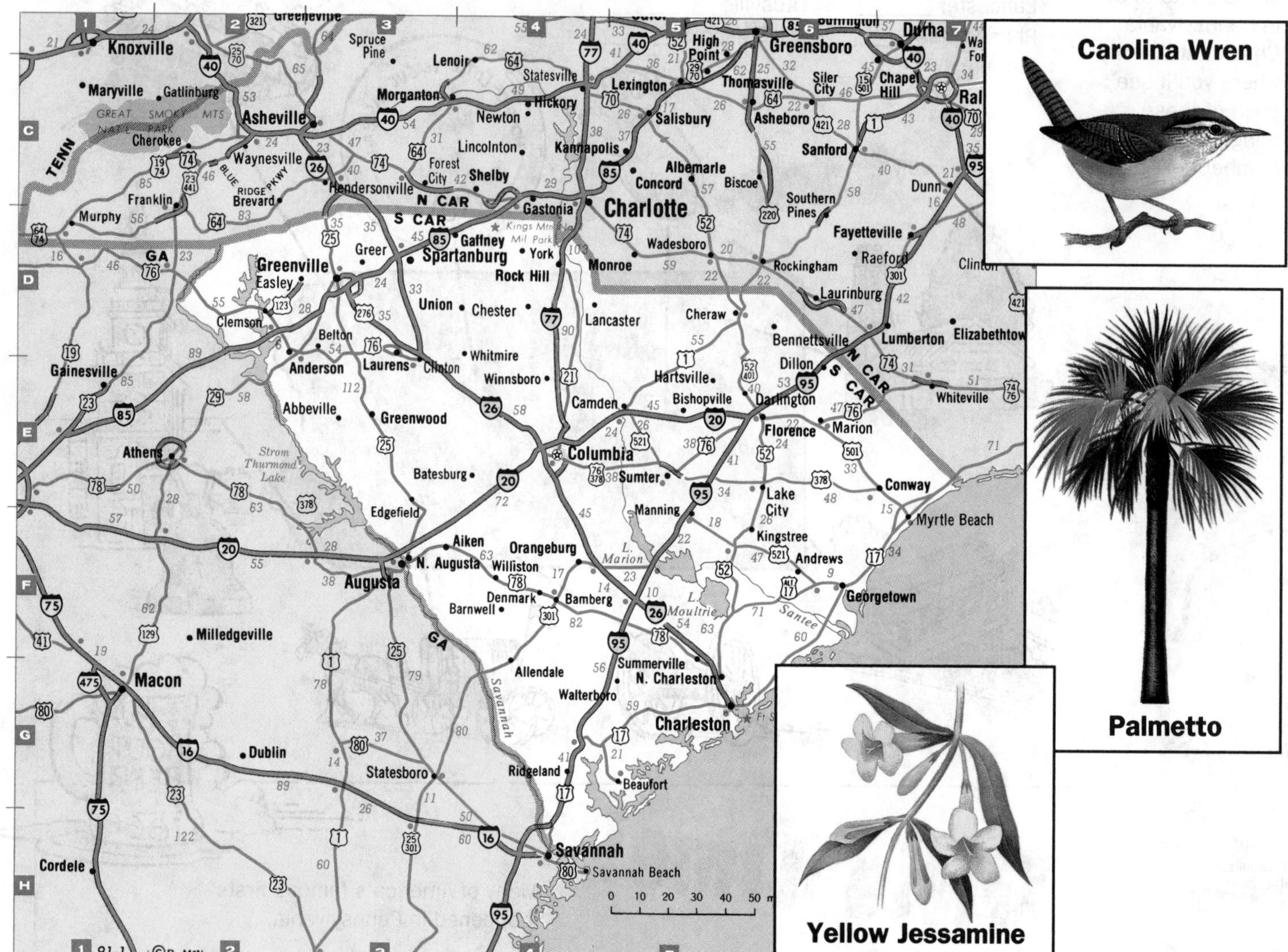

Carolina Wren

Palmetto

Yellow Jessamine

Super Sleuth!

LION

CAR

How many words are hiding in the name

SOUTH CAROLINA

Randy found 100. How many can you find?

____

____

____

____

____

____

SOUTH DAKOTA

Capital: Pierre

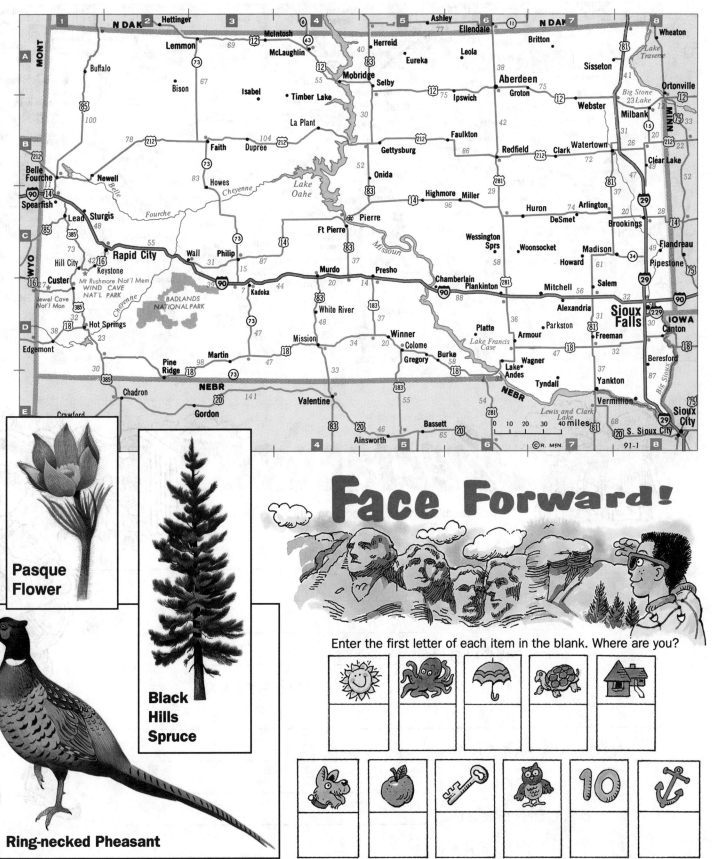

Pasque Flower

Black Hills Spruce

Ring-necked Pheasant

Face Forward!

Enter the first letter of each item in the blank. Where are you?

				10	

TENNESSEE

Capital: Nashville

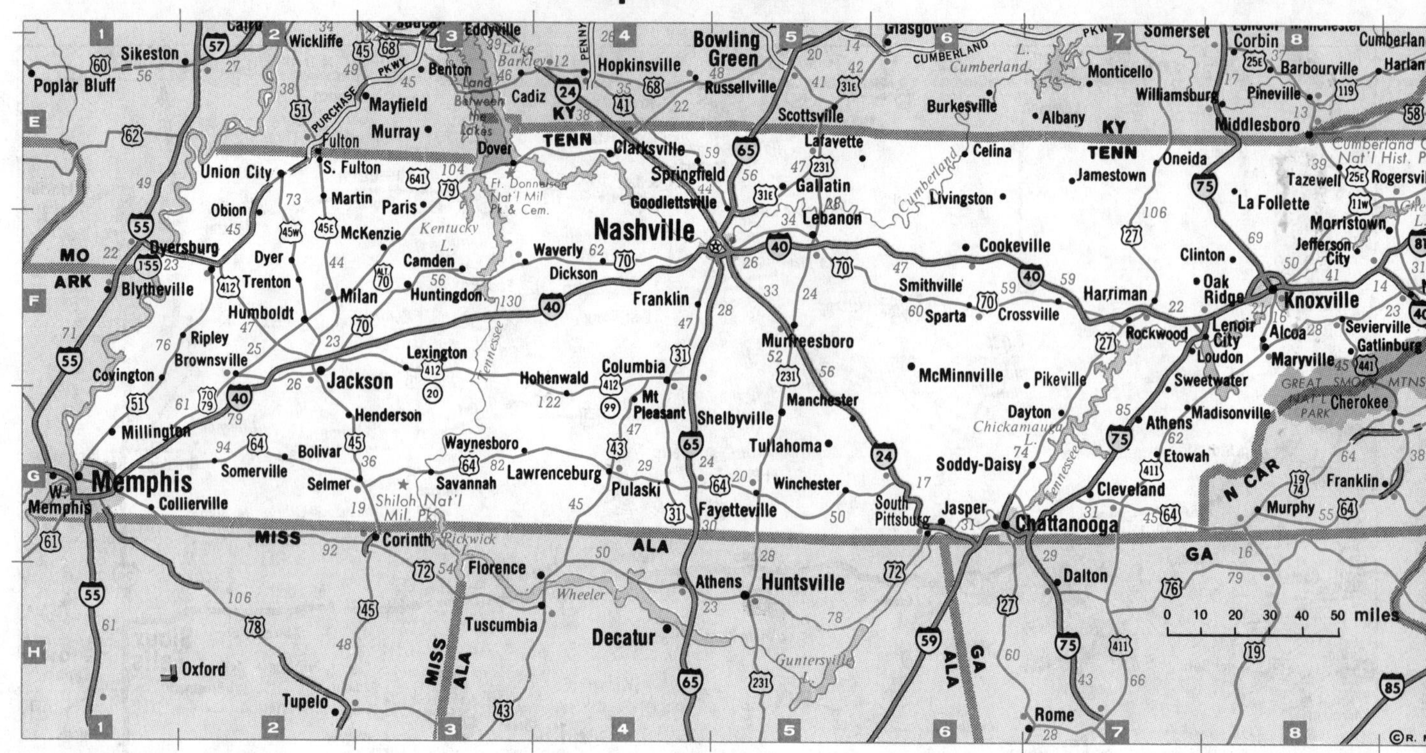

Spectacular!

Unscramble these cool vacation places in Tennessee.

NGRDA LEO YPRO ____________ ____________

ELLASHNIV __________________

LACEGRAND __________________

PHEMSIM ______________

TEGAR MYOSK UNMOSTIAN

__________ __________ __________________

GOONATATCHA ______________________

LIVEKLONX __________________

BALTNIGRUG ____________________

LYDOPRAN ________________

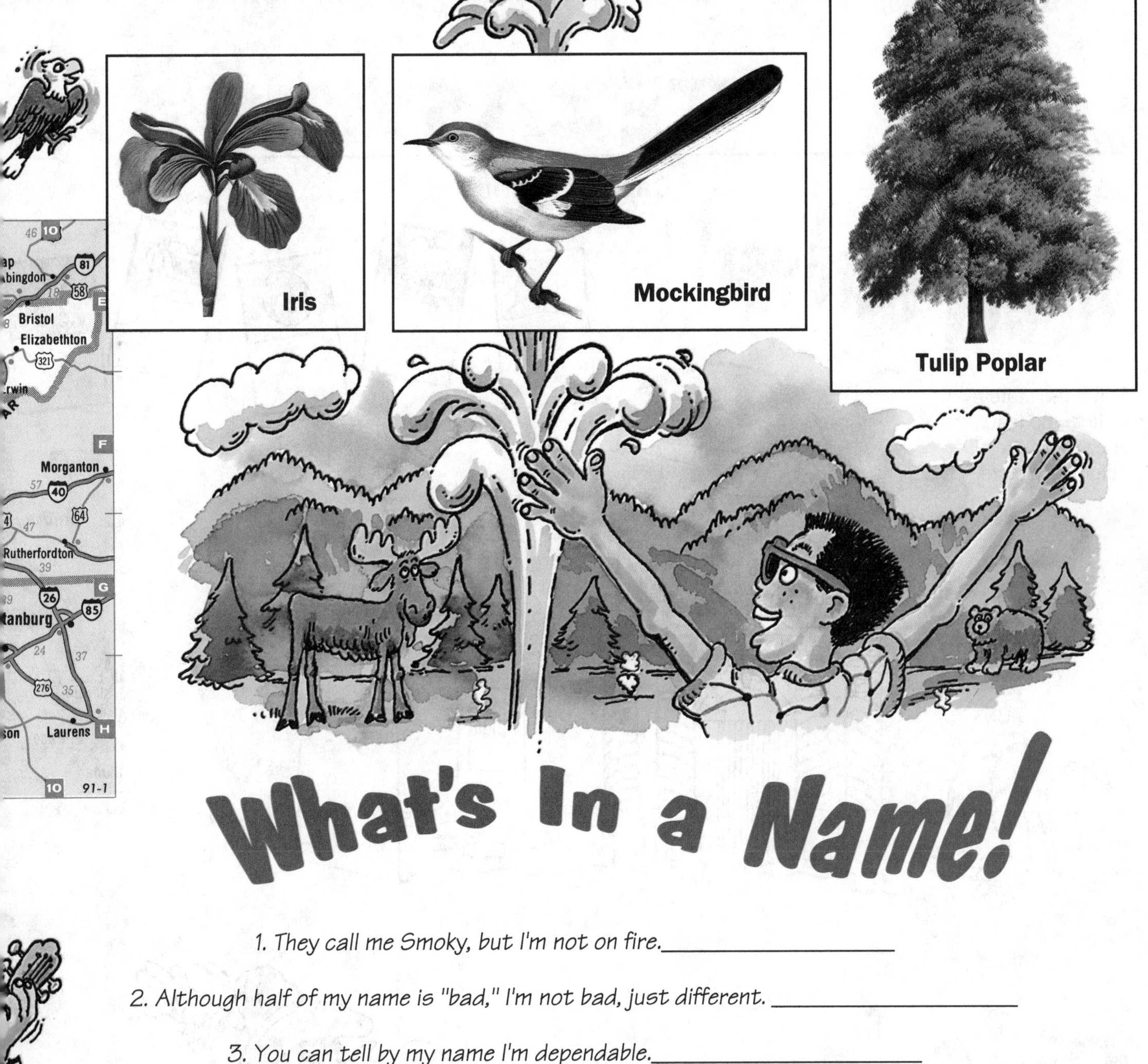

What's In a Name!

1. They call me Smoky, but I'm not on fire.__________________

2. Although half of my name is "bad," I'm not bad, just different. __________________

3. You can tell by my name I'm dependable.__________________

4. I'm almost filled with salt, but you can't pour me out. __________________

5. I'm the only capitol building with an oil well underneath. __________________

6. My name says I'm golden, but I'm not made of gold. __________________

7. I'm mammoth, but I'm not a mountain. __________________

8. I'm a happy state. __________________

9. According to my name I have four legs, a large head, and roamed the prairies many years ago. Instead, I'm a city. __________________

10. I'm not a pebble, I'm a city. __________________

11. I could be a sweet roll, but I'm not. I'm a state capital. __________________

12. I was named for the first president of the United States. __________________

TEXAS

Capital: Austin

Howdy Pardner!

Name the state by writing the last letter of each picture clue. Color the picture.

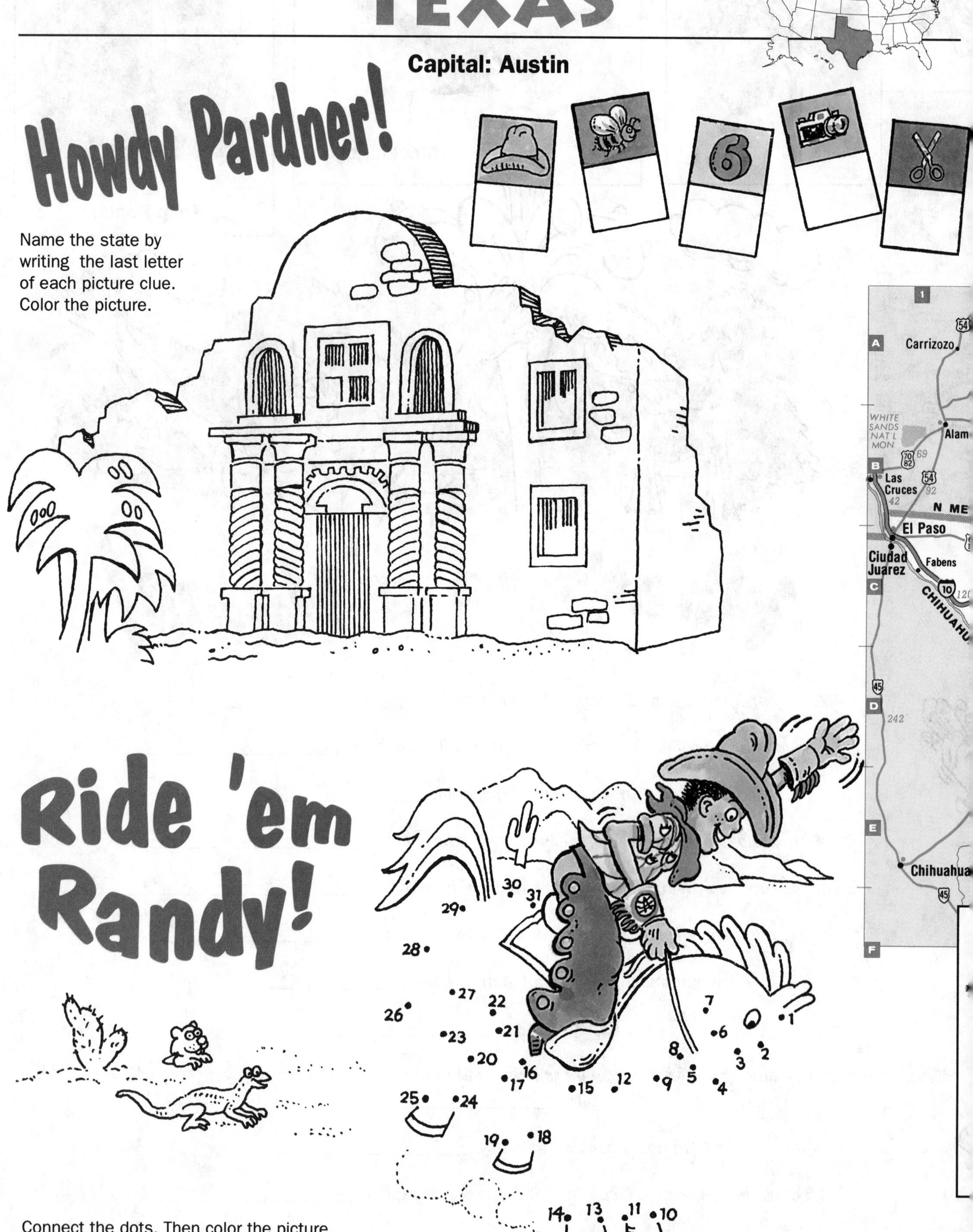

Ride 'em Randy!

Connect the dots. Then color the picture.

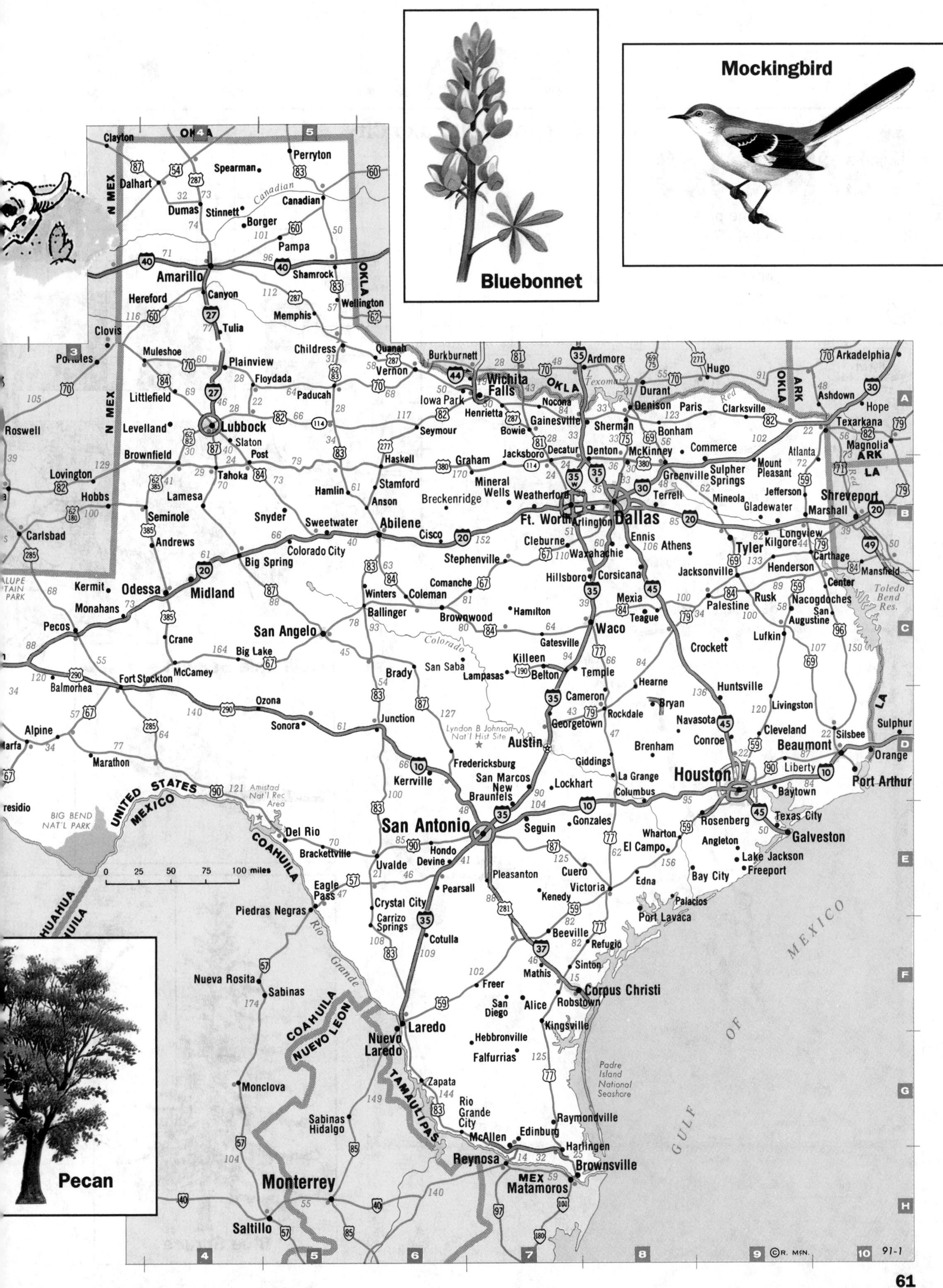
Mockingbird
Bluebonnet
Pecan
OKLA
N MEX
ARK
LA
MEX
UNITED STATES
MEXICO
COAHUILA
NUEVO LEON
TAMAULIPAS
GULF OF MEXICO
Clayton
Perryton
Spearman
Dalhart
Canadian
Dumas
Stinnett
Borger
Pampa
Amarillo
Shamrock
Hereford
Canyon
Wellington
Memphis
Tulia
Clovis
Portales
Muleshoe
Plainview
Childress
Quanah
Vernon
Burkburnett
Wichita Falls
Ardmore
Hugo
Arkadelphia
Floydada
Paducah
Iowa Park
Durant
Ashdown
Littlefield
Lubbock
Henrietta
Nocona
Denison
Paris
Clarksville
Hope
Roswell
Levelland
Slaton
Seymour
Gainesville
Sherman
Bowie
Bonham
Texarkana
Brownfield
Post
Haskell
Graham
Jacksboro
Decatur
Denton
McKinney
Commerce
Atlanta
Magnolia
Lovington
Tahoka
Mineral Wells
Greenville
Sulpher Springs
Mount Pleasant
Lamesa
Stamford
Hamlin
Weatherford
Terrell
Mineola
Jefferson
Hobbs
Anson
Breckenridge
Gladewater
Shreveport
Seminole
Snyder
Sweetwater
Abilene
Ft. Worth
Arlington
Dallas
Marshall
Carlsbad
Andrews
Cisco
Cleburne
Ennis
Athens
Tyler
Longview
Kilgore
Colorado City
Waxahachie
Carthage
Big Spring
Stephenville
Jacksonville
Henderson
Mansfield
Kermit
Odessa
Midland
Comanche
Hillsboro
Corsicana
Center
Toledo Bend Res.
Winters
Coleman
Mexia
Palestine
Rusk
Nacogdoches
Monahans
Ballinger
Brownwood
Hamilton
Teague
San Augustine
Pecos
San Angelo
Crane
Waco
Lufkin
Gatesville
Crockett
Big Lake
Killeen
Belton
Temple
McCamey
San Saba
Lampasas
Brady
Hearne
Fort Stockton
Balmorhea
Huntsville
Ozona
Cameron
Bryan
Livingston
Rockdale
Navasota
Alpine
Junction
Georgetown
Sonora
Conroe
Cleveland
Sulphur
Silsbee
Marfa
Lyndon B Johnson Nat'l Hist Site
Austin
Brenham
Beaumont
Orange
Marathon
Giddings
Houston
Liberty
Fredericksburg
Port Arthur
Kerrville
San Marcos
La Grange
Lockhart
New Braunfels
Columbus
Baytown
Presidio
Amistad Nat'l Rec Area
BIG BEND NAT'L PARK
Del Rio
San Antonio
Seguin
Gonzales
Rosenberg
Texas City
Galveston
Wharton
El Campo
Angleton
Brackettville
Hondo
Uvalde
Devine
Cuero
Lake Jackson
Freeport
Pleasanton
Bay City
Eagle Pass
Pearsall
Victoria
Edna
Crystal City
Kenedy
Palacios
Piedras Negras
Carrizo Springs
Port Lavaca
Beeville
Cotulla
Refugio
Sinton
Nueva Rosita
Mathis
Sabinas
Freer
Corpus Christi
San Diego
Alice
Robstown
Laredo
Nuevo Laredo
Kingsville
Hebbronville
Falfurrias
Padre Island National Seashore
Monclova
Zapata
Rio Grande City
Raymondville
Sabinas Hidalgo
McAllen
Edinburg
Harlingen
Reynosa
Brownsville
Monterrey
Matamoros
Saltillo
Rio Grande
Colorado
Canadian
Red
Texoma
0 25 50 75 100 miles
©R. McN.
91-1

UTAH

Capital: Salt Lake City

Park Pics!

Utah has many awesome parks. Fill in the names in the puzzle, and then help Randy find them on the map.

Arches	Capitol Reef	Rainbow Bridge
Bryce Canyon	Cedar Breaks	Zion
Canyonlands	Dinosaur	

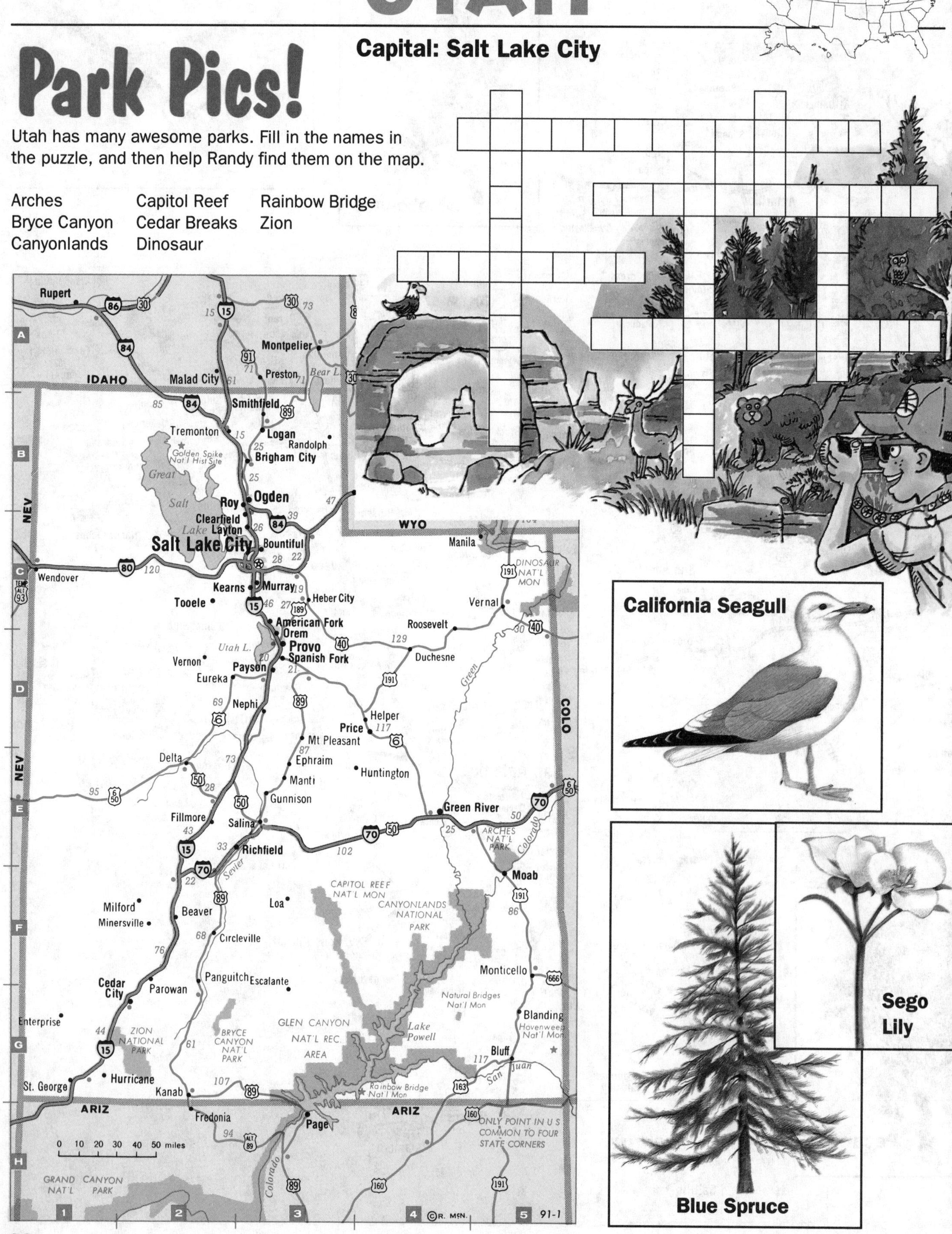

VERMONT

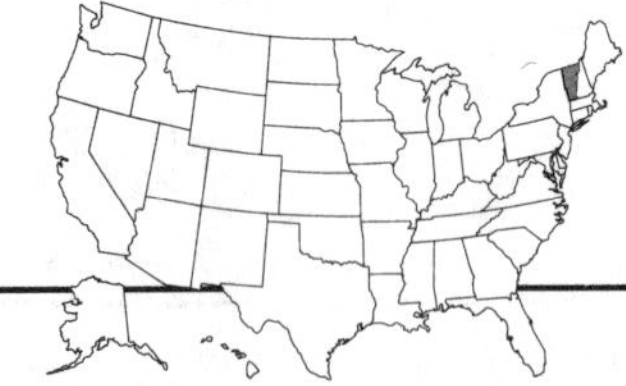

Capital: Montpelier

Red Clover

Hermit Thrush

Sugar Maple

Help Randy find the right ski trail to the bottom of the mountain!

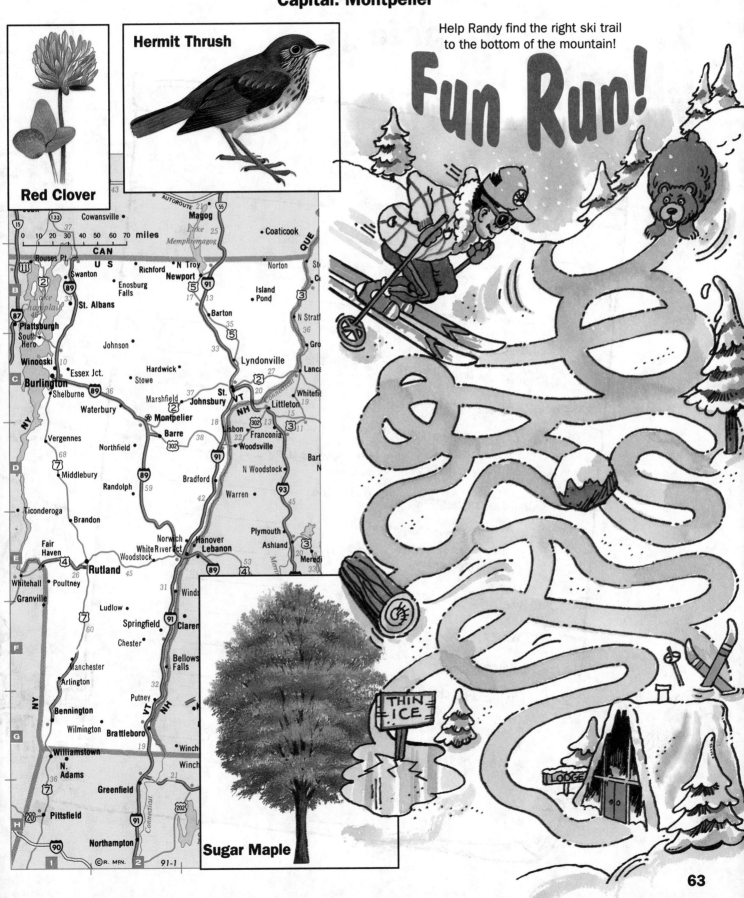

Fun Run!

THIN ICE

LODGE

VIRGINIA

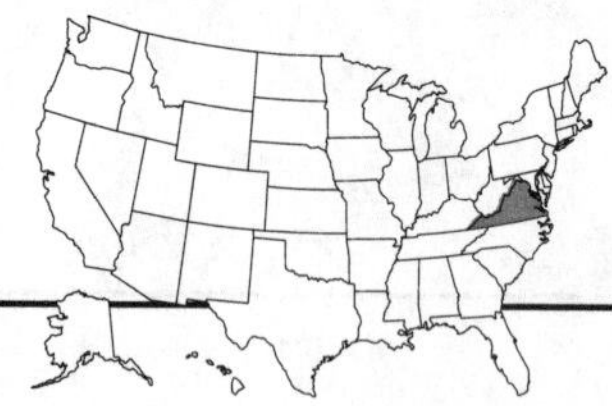

Capital: Richmond

Discover America!

1. What four States meet at one corner? ____________, ____________, ____________, ____________
2. What states border on Lake Michigan? ____________, ____________, ____________, ____________
3. What is the longest river in the United States? ____________
4. What is the largest state in area in the U.S.? ____________
5. What is the smallest state in area in the U.S.? ____________
6. What is the highest city in the U.S.? ____________
7. What is the oldest National Park in the U.S.? ____________
8. What is the highest point in the U.S.? ____________
9. What is the lowest point in the U.S.? ____________
10. What is the largest lake in the U.S. ? ____________
11. Where can you see the Liberty Bell? ____________
12. Where is the Golden Gate Bridge? ____________
13. Where can you see Mount Rushmore? ____________
14. What was the first state to enter the union? ____________
15. What was the 50th state in the U.S.? ____________
16. What state is called the "Mother of Presidents"? ____________

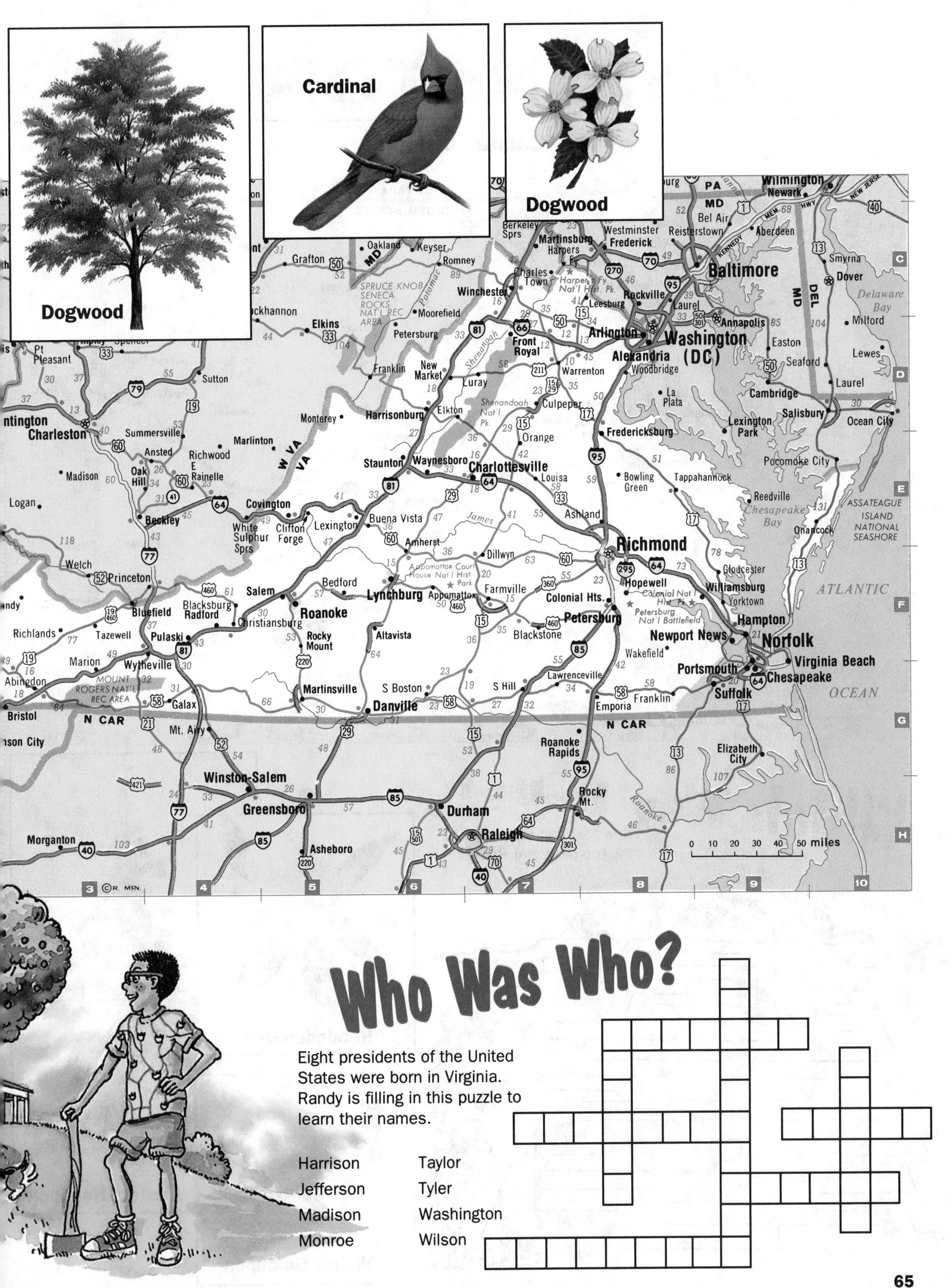

Who Was Who?

Eight presidents of the United States were born in Virginia. Randy is filling in this puzzle to learn their names.

Harrison	Taylor
Jefferson	Tyler
Madison	Washington
Monroe	Wilson

WASHINGTON

Capital: Olympia

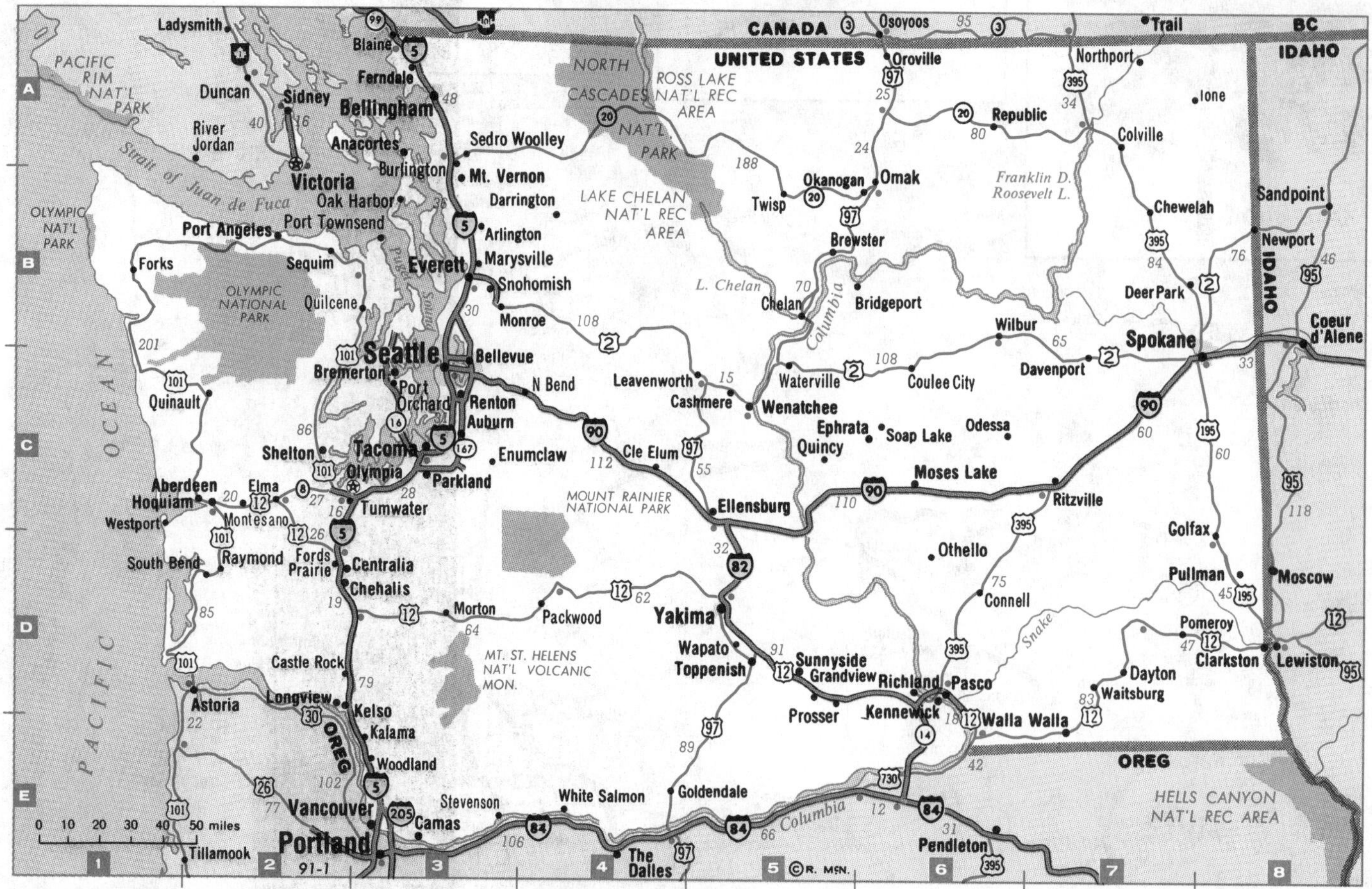

CANADA
UNITED STATES
BC
IDAHO
OREG
PACIFIC OCEAN
PACIFIC RIM NAT'L PARK
OLYMPIC NAT'L PARK
OLYMPIC NATIONAL PARK
NORTH CASCADES NAT'L PARK
ROSS LAKE NAT'L REC AREA
LAKE CHELAN NAT'L REC AREA
MOUNT RAINIER NATIONAL PARK
MT. ST. HELENS NAT'L VOLCANIC MON.
HELLS CANYON NAT'L REC AREA
Strait of Juan de Fuca
Franklin D. Roosevelt L.
L. Chelan
Columbia
Snake
Ladysmith
Duncan
Sidney
River Jordan
Victoria
Blaine
Ferndale
Bellingham
Anacortes
Burlington
Sedro Woolley
Mt. Vernon
Darrington
Oak Harbor
Port Angeles
Port Townsend
Arlington
Forks
Sequim
Everett
Marysville
Snohomish
Quilcene
Monroe
Seattle
Bellevue
Bremerton
Port Orchard
Renton
Auburn
N Bend
Quinault
Shelton
Tacoma
Olympia
Enumclaw
Parkland
Aberdeen
Hoquiam
Elma
Montesano
Tumwater
Westport
South Bend
Raymond
Fords Prairie
Centralia
Chehalis
Morton
Packwood
Castle Rock
Astoria
Longview
Kelso
Kalama
Woodland
Vancouver
Portland
Camas
Stevenson
White Salmon
Tillamook
The Dalles
Goldendale
Osoyoos
Oroville
Trail
Northport
Ione
Republic
Colville
Okanogan
Omak
Twisp
Brewster
Chewelah
Sandpoint
Newport
Deer Park
Chelan
Bridgeport
Wilbur
Spokane
Coeur d'Alene
Leavenworth
Cashmere
Waterville
Wenatchee
Coulee City
Davenport
Ephrata
Soap Lake
Odessa
Quincy
Cle Elum
Ellensburg
Moses Lake
Ritzville
Othello
Golfax
Pullman
Moscow
Yakima
Wapato
Toppenish
Sunnyside
Grandview
Connell
Pomeroy
Clarkston
Lewiston
Dayton
Waitsburg
Richland
Pasco
Prosser
Kennewick
Walla Walla
Pendleton
0 10 20 30 40 50 miles
©R. McN.
91-1

Which Way Is Up!

How fast can Randy get to the top of Mount Rainier?

Rhododendron

Willow Goldfinch

Western Hemlock

WEST VIRGINIA

Capital: Charleston

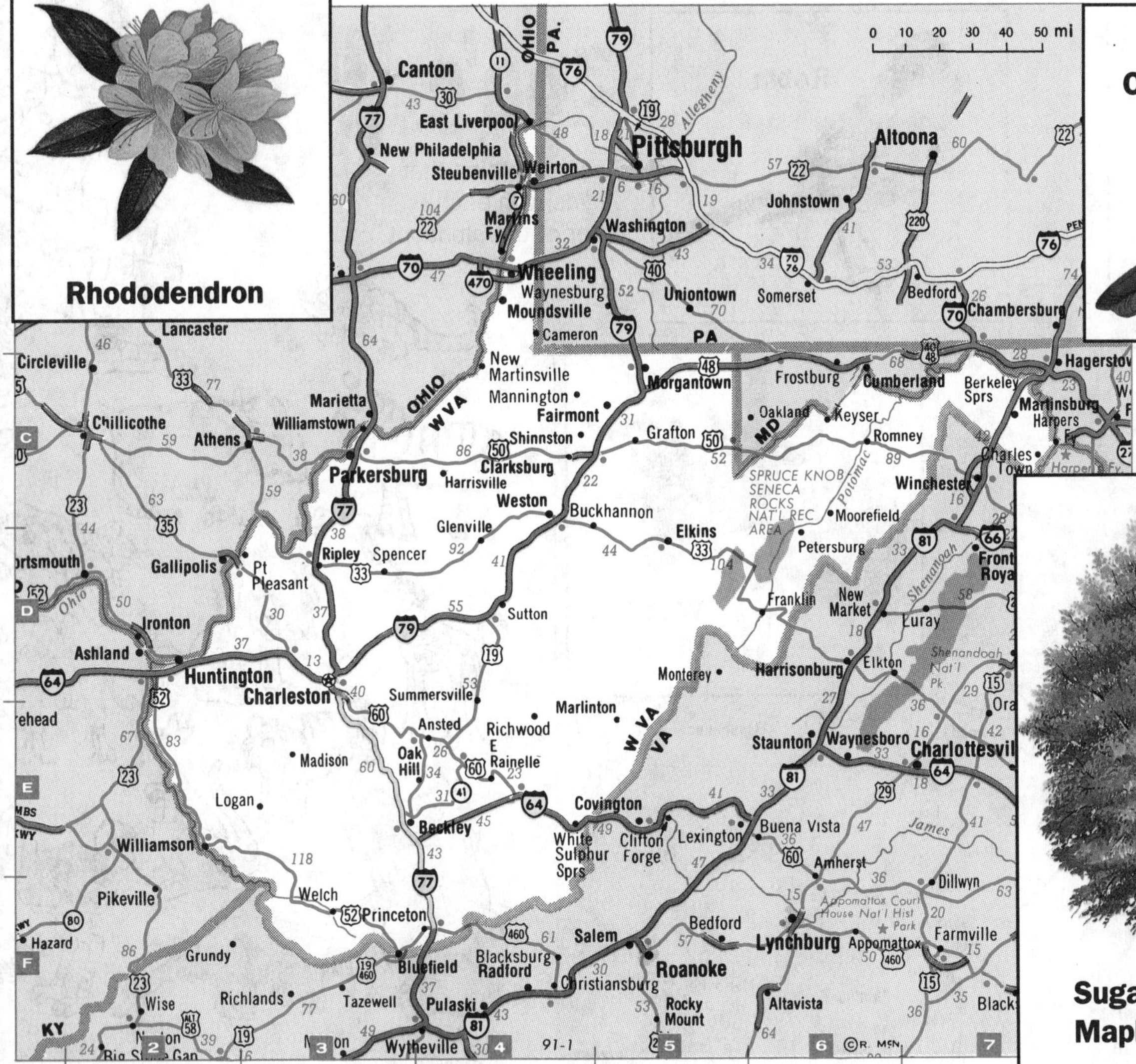

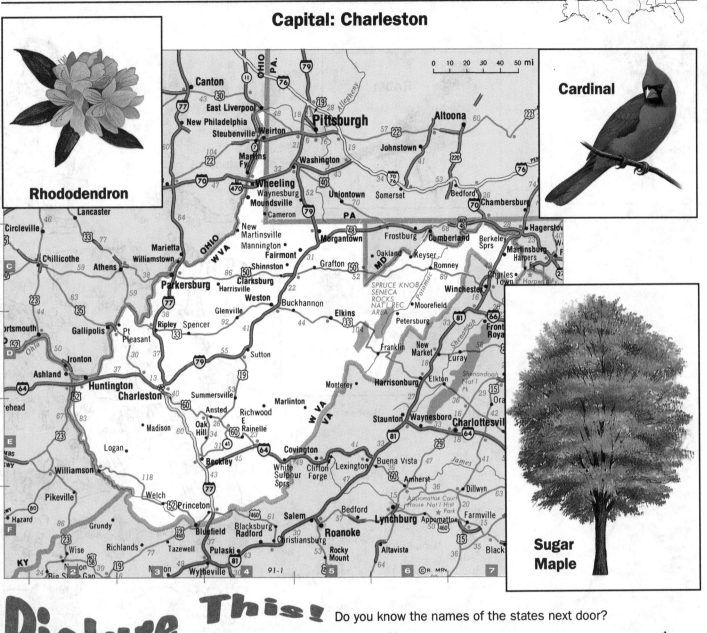

Rhododendron

Cardinal

Sugar Maple

Picture This!

Do you know the names of the states next door?

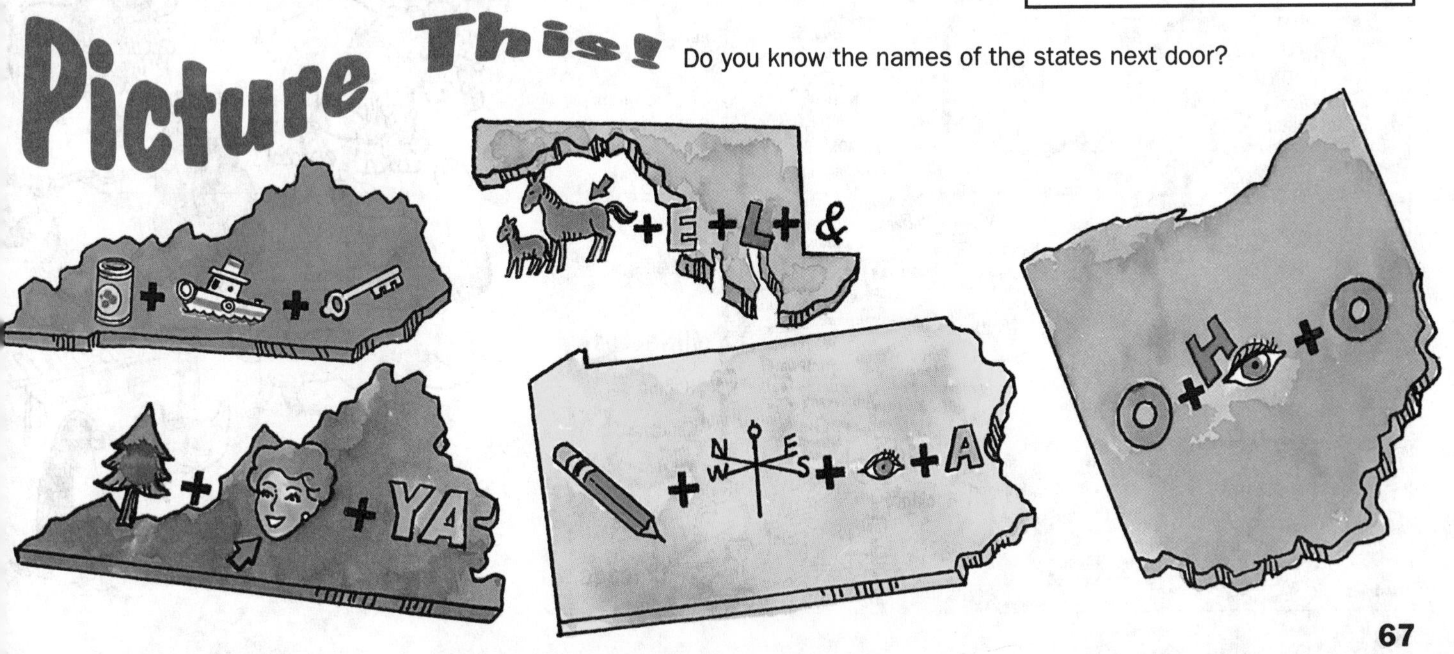

Sugar Maple

WISCONSIN

Capital: Madison

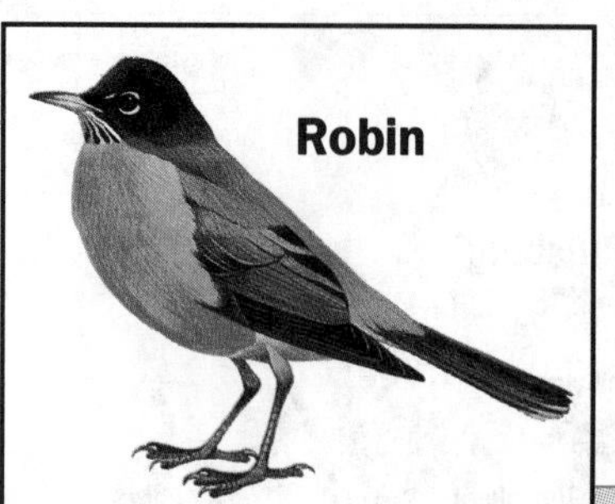

Robin

Wood Violet

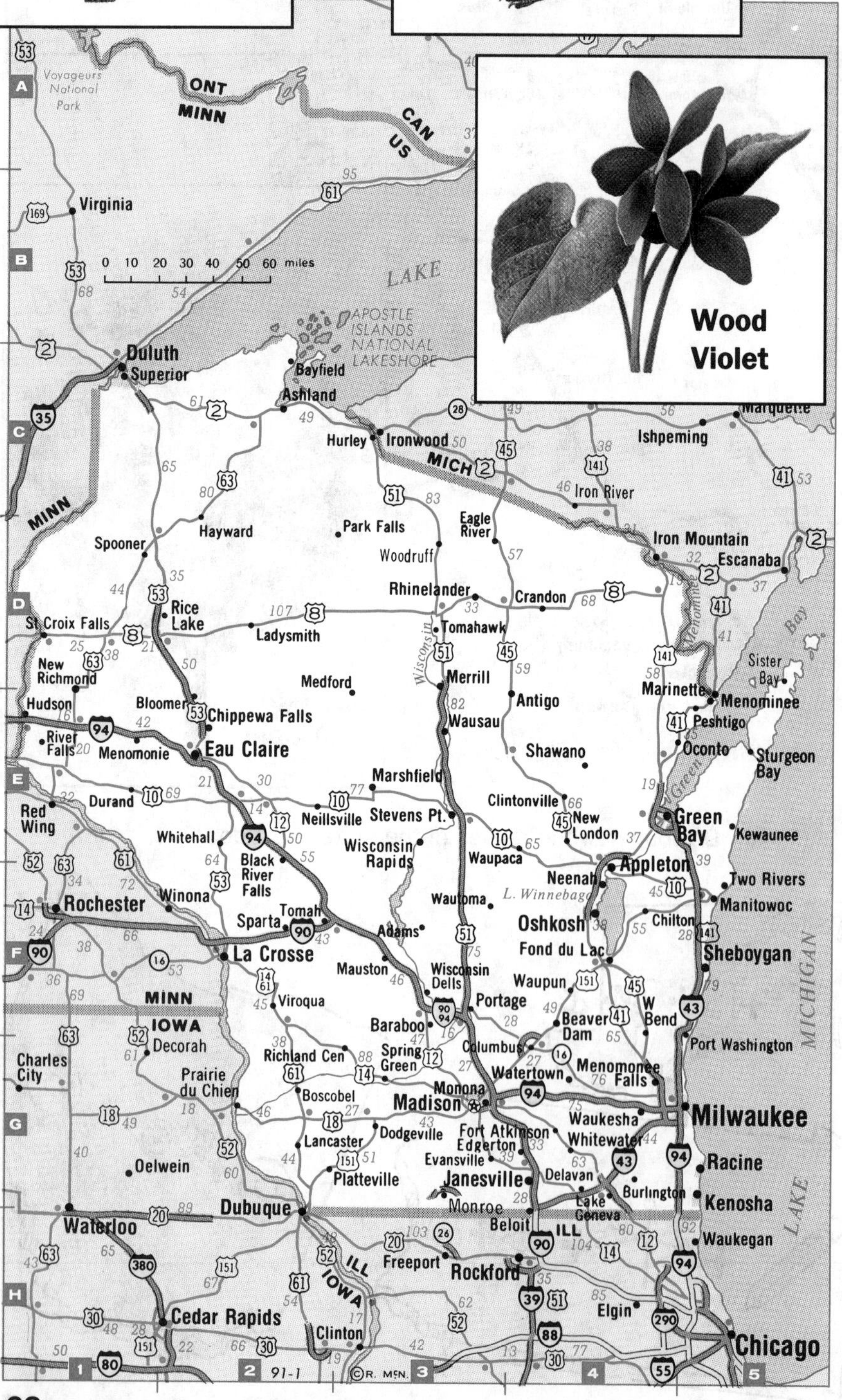

Zoo's Who!

Find something that begins with each letter of the alphabet.

Indian Paintbrush

WYOMING

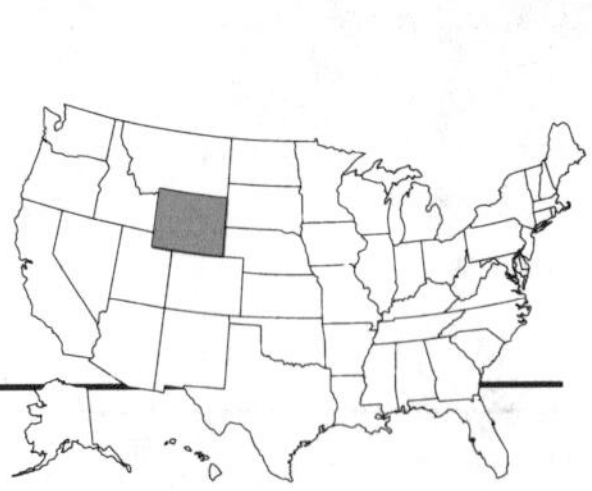

Capital: Cheyenne

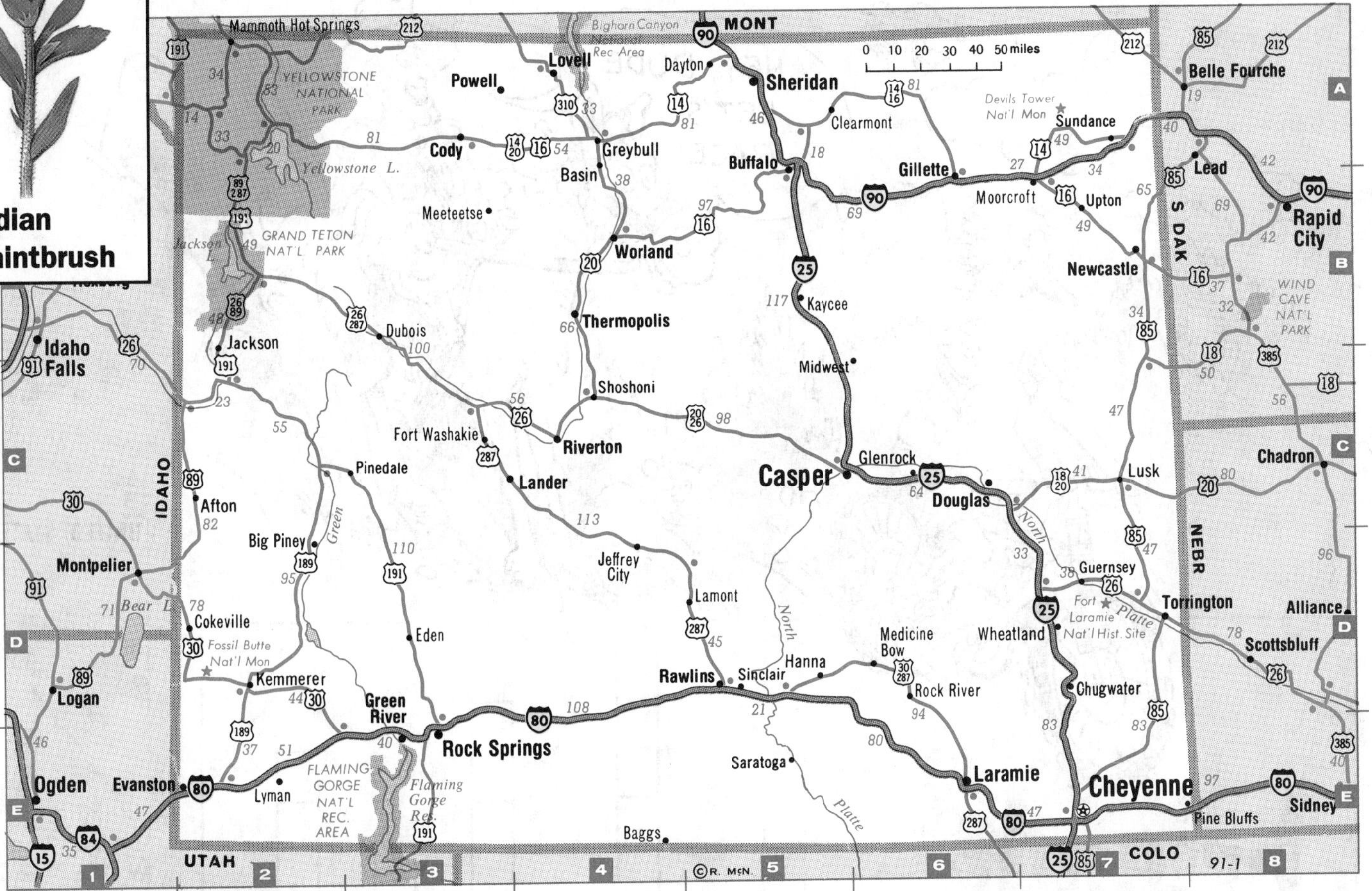

MONT
Mammoth Hot Springs
YELLOWSTONE NATIONAL PARK
Yellowstone L.
GRAND TETON NAT'L PARK
Bighorn Canyon Nat'l Rec Area
Lovell
Powell
Dayton
Sheridan
Cody
Greybull
Basin
Buffalo
Clearmont
Gillette
Moorcroft
Devils Tower Nat'l Mon
Sundance
Upton
Belle Fourche
Lead
Rapid City
Meeteetse
Worland
Thermopolis
Kaycee
Newcastle
WIND CAVE NAT'L PARK
Idaho Falls
Jackson
Dubois
Midwest
Shoshoni
Fort Washakie
Riverton
Lander
Pinedale
Afton
Casper
Glenrock
Douglas
Lusk
Chadron
IDAHO
S DAK
NEBR
Big Piney
Montpelier
Jeffrey City
Lamont
Guernsey
Torrington
Fort Laramie Nat'l Hist Site
Alliance
Scottsbluff
Cokeville
Fossil Butte Nat'l Mon
Eden
Medicine Bow
Wheatland
Hanna
Logan
Kemmerer
Green River
Rawlins
Sinclair
Rock River
Chugwater
Rock Springs
Saratoga
Laramie
Ogden
Evanston
Lyman
FLAMING GORGE NAT'L REC. AREA
Flaming Gorge Res.
Cheyenne
Pine Bluffs
Sidney
Baggs
UTAH
COLO
Green
North Platte
0 10 20 30 40 50 miles
©R. McN.
91-1

Cottonwood

Meadowlark

Snow Time!

What is Randy taking on his winter vacation?

SK
4
OF
MIT
W

CANADA

Capital: Ottawa

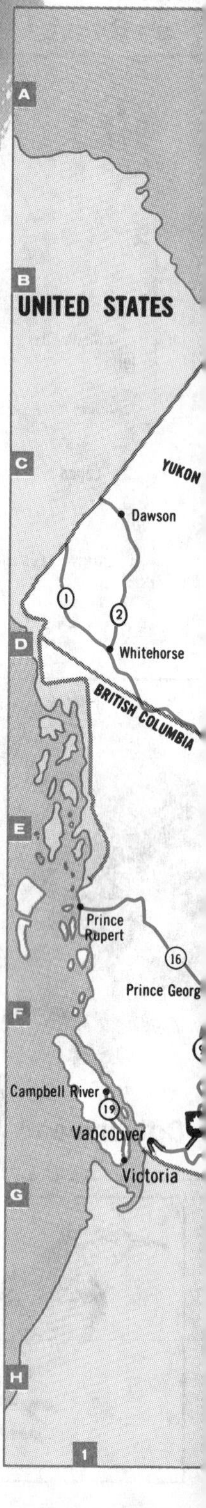

Friends Next Door

Fill in the province names
Alberta
British Columbia
Manitoba
New Brunswick
Newfoundland
Nova Scotia
Ontario
Prince Edward Island
Québec
Saskatchewan
Yukon

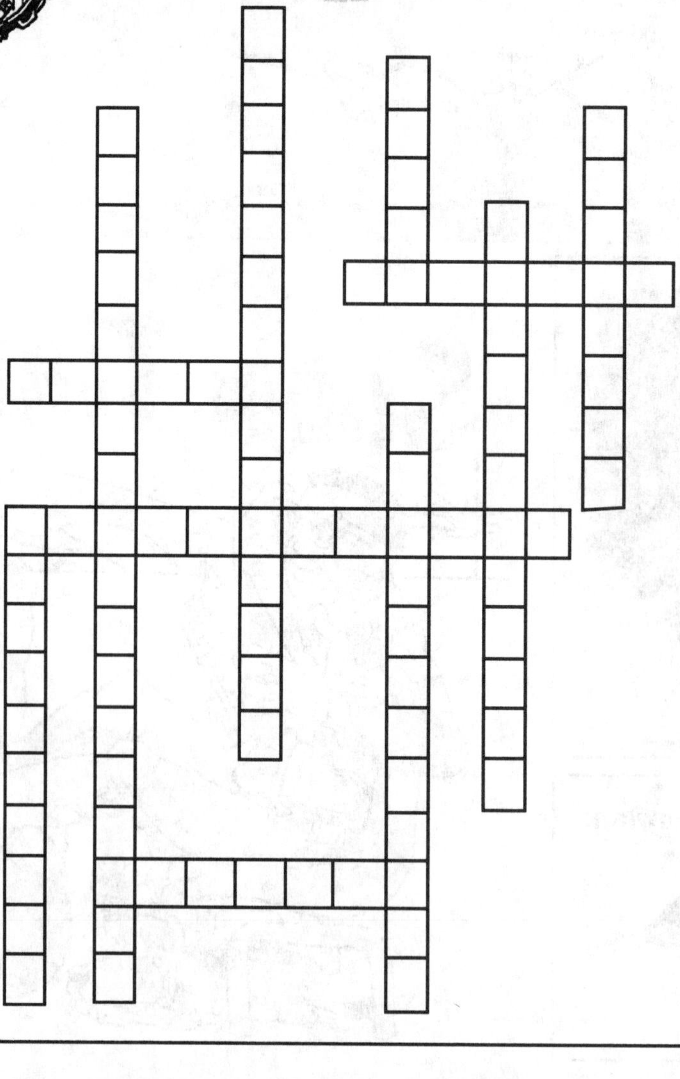

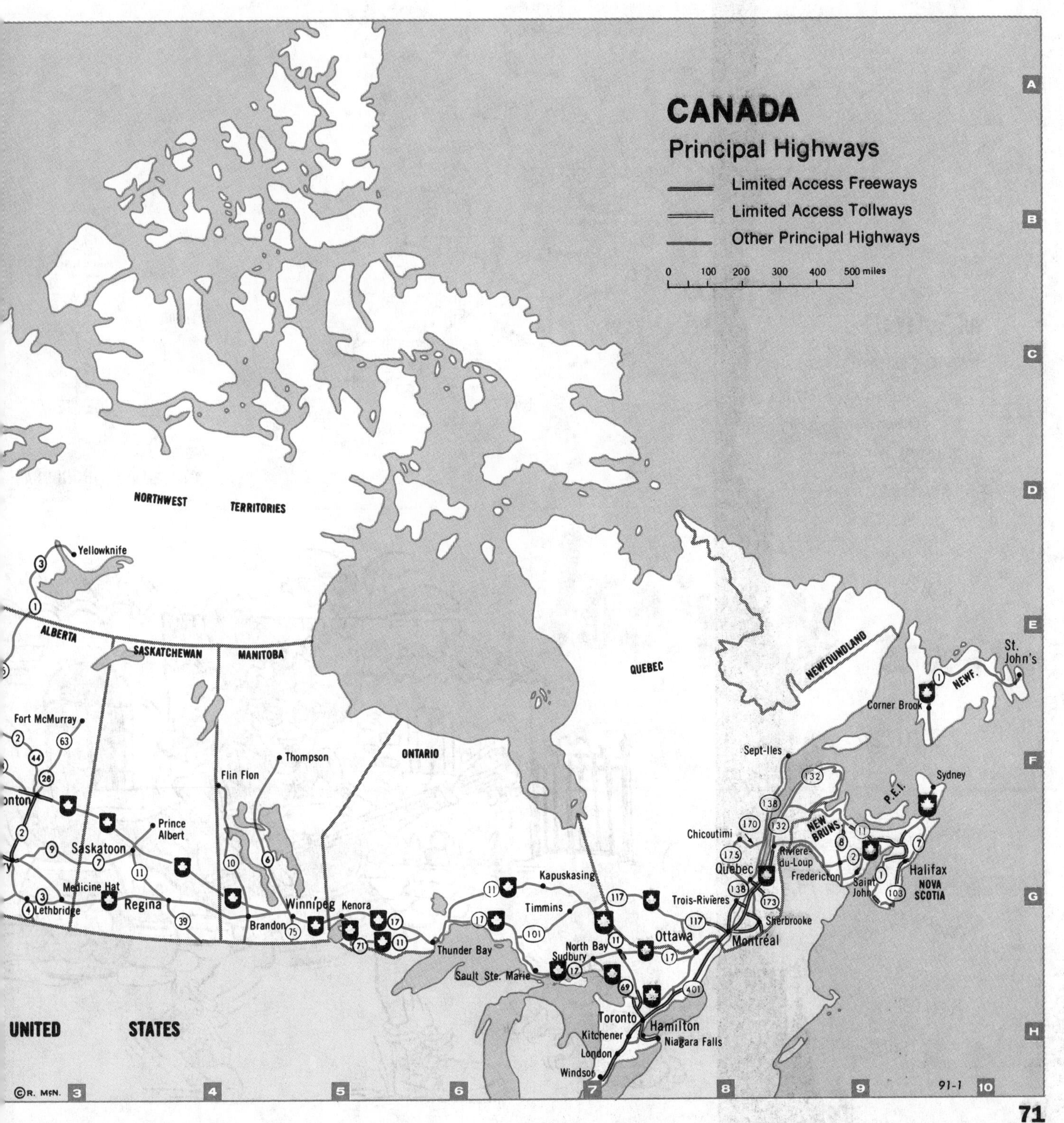
CANADA
Principal Highways
Limited Access Freeways
Limited Access Tollways
Other Principal Highways
0 100 200 300 400 500 miles
NORTHWEST TERRITORIES
Yellowknife
ALBERTA
SASKATCHEWAN
MANITOBA
ONTARIO
QUEBEC
NEWFOUNDLAND
NEWF.
St. John's
Corner Brook
Sept-Iles
Sydney
P.E.I.
NEW BRUNS.
NOVA SCOTIA
Halifax
Saint John
Fredericton
Rivière-du-Loup
Chicoutimi
Quebec
Trois-Rivières
Sherbrooke
Montréal
Ottawa
North Bay
Sudbury
Sault Ste. Marie
Toronto
Hamilton
Niagara Falls
Kitchener
London
Windsor
Kapuskasing
Timmins
Thunder Bay
Kenora
Winnipeg
Brandon
Thompson
Flin Flon
Prince Albert
Saskatoon
Regina
Medicine Hat
Lethbridge
Fort McMurray
UNITED STATES
©R. McN.
91-1

MEXICO

Capital: Mexico City

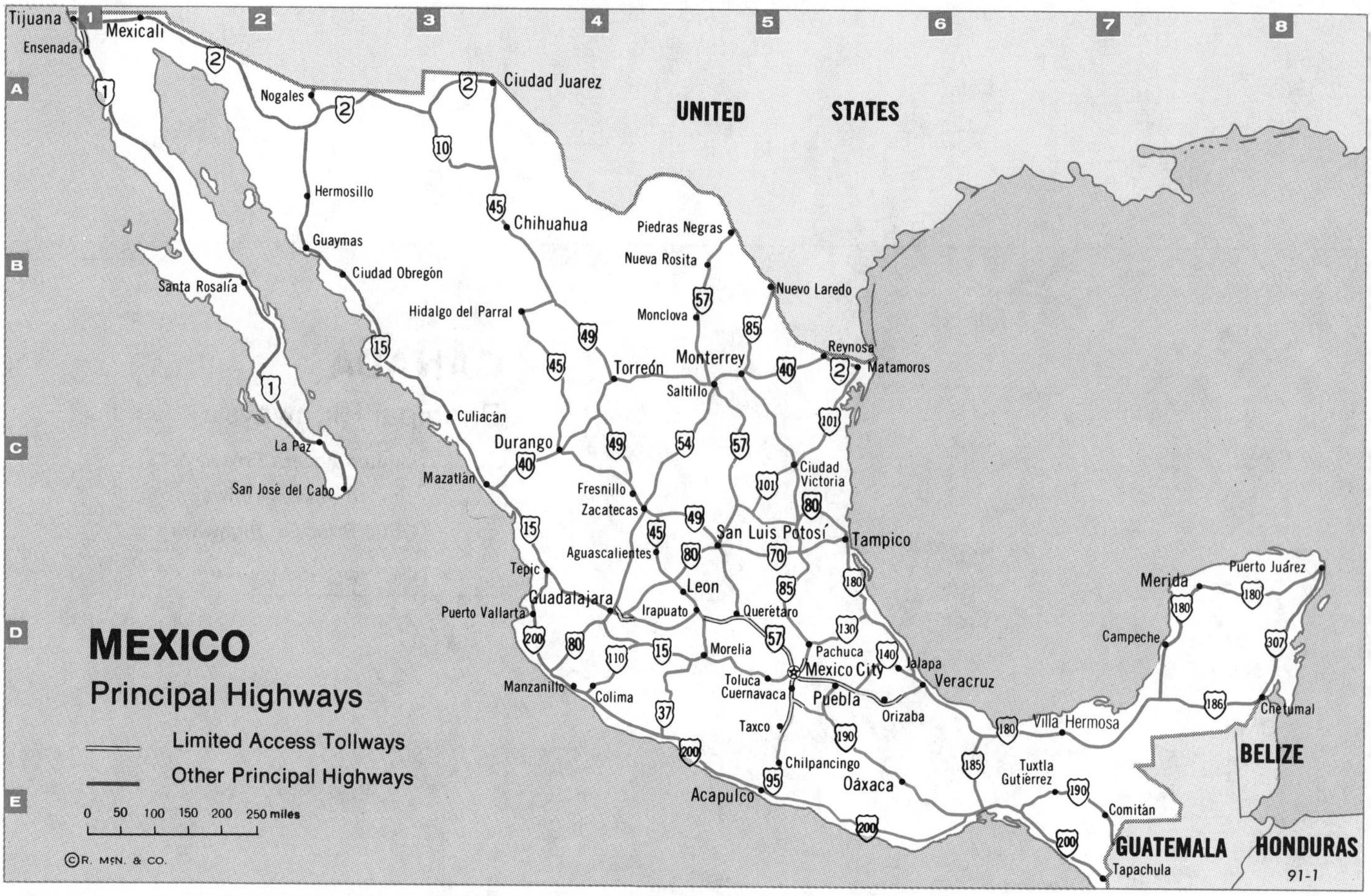

MEXICO
Principal Highways

Limited Access Tollways
Other Principal Highways

0 50 100 150 200 250 miles

©R. McN. & CO.

Tijuana, Ensenada, Mexicali, Nogales, Ciudad Juarez, UNITED STATES, Hermosillo, Chihuahua, Guaymas, Ciudad Obregón, Santa Rosalía, Piedras Negras, Nueva Rosita, Nuevo Laredo, Hidalgo del Parral, Monclova, Torreón, Monterrey, Reynosa, Matamoros, Saltillo, Culiacán, La Paz, San José del Cabo, Durango, Mazatlán, Fresnillo, Zacatecas, Ciudad Victoria, San Luis Potosí, Tampico, Aguascalientes, Tepic, Leon, Guadalajara, Irapuato, Querétaro, Puerto Vallarta, Morelia, Pachuca, Mexico City, Jalapa, Veracruz, Toluca, Cuernavaca, Puebla, Orizaba, Manzanillo, Colima, Taxco, Chilpancingo, Oáxaca, Acapulco, Merida, Puerto Juárez, Campeche, Villa Hermosa, Chetumal, BELIZE, Tuxtla Gutiérrez, Comitán, GUATEMALA, HONDURAS, Tapachula

91-1

Hola (Hi)

Viva Mexico!

Hasta luego (See Ya)

¿Que pasa? (What's Happening?)

¡Fantástico! (Awesome!)

Mañana (Later Dude)

ANSWER PAGE

CAPITALS (page 8)

32. New York
20. Maryland
10. Georgia
19. Maine
43. Texas
18. Louisiana
34. North Dakota
12. Idaho
21. Massachusetts
28. Nevada
48. West Virginia
50. Wyoming
40. South Carolina
35. Ohio
29. New Hampshire
6. Colorado
15. Iowa
8. Delaware
17. Kentucky
38. Pennsylvania
7. Connecticut
26. Montana
11. Hawaii
14. Indiana
24. Mississippi
25. Missouri
2. Alaska
22. Michigan
27. Nebraska
4. Arkansas
49. Wisconsin
1. Alabama
45. Vermont
42. Tennessee
36. Oklahoma
47. Washington
3. Arizona
41. South Dakota
39. Rhode Island
33. North Carolina
46. Virginia
5. California
23. Minnesota
37. Oregon
44. Utah
31. New Mexico
13. Illinois
9. Florida
16. Kansas
30. New Jersey

ALABAMA (page 10)

		M	O	N	T	G	O	M	E	R	Y
N								U			
A	Z	A	L	E	A	S		S	H	I	P
T			A		R		S	E	A		
U			K		E			U			P
R	A	C	E	C	A	R		M	I	L	L
A				A		O			V		A
L				V		C	A	N	Y	O	N
B		W		E		K					T
R		A				E			Z		A
I		T	E	E		T		F	O	R	T
D		E					M		O		I
G	A	R	D	E	N		A				O
E		F			E		L		R		N
	C	A	P	I	T	O	L		A		
		L		N					C		
H	E	L	E	N	K	E	L	L	E	R	

ARKANSAS (page 13)

Tennessee
Louisiana
Mississippi
Kentucky
Missouri
Oklahoma
Texas

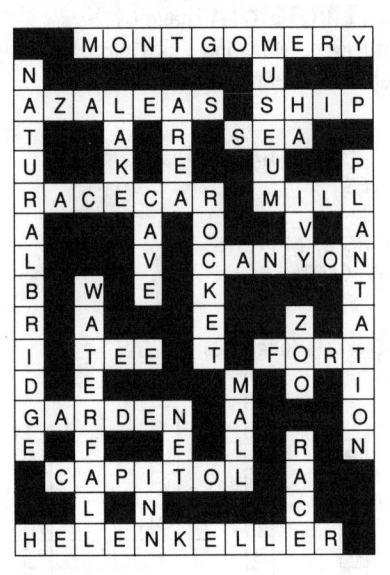

CALIFORNIA (page 14)

Riddles
1. Eureka
2. Twentynine Palms
3. Santa Cruz
4. Bakersfield

California is Wild
9. Vallejo
4. Oakland

8. San Francisco
3. Monterey
10. Santa Barbara
2. Los Angeles
5. Palm Springs
1. Escondido
7. San Diego (Sea World)
6. San Diego (Zoo)

GEORGIA (page 20)

N	X	Z	A	L	A	B	A	M	A	X	Y	A
Y	O	Y	X	Y	X	Y	Y	X	Z	Y	N	X
X	Z	R	Z	Y	Y	Z	X	Y	Y	I	Y	Z
G	Z	Y	T	X	Z	X	Z	X	L	Z	X	F
E	Y	X	Z	H	X	Z	Y	O	X	Y	X	L
O	Z	Y	Z	Y	C	Y	R	Y	Z	X	Y	O
R	Y	Z	X	Y	Z	A	Z	X	Y	Z	X	R
G	X	Y	Y	Z	C	X	R	Y	X	Z	Y	I
I	Y	Z	X	H	Y	Z	Y	O	Z	Y	X	D
A	Z	X	T	Z	Y	X	Z	Y	L	Y	Z	A
Z	X	U	Y	X	Z	Y	X	Y	X	I	Y	X
X	O	X	Z	Y	Z	X	Z	Z	X	Z	N	Z
S	X	T	E	N	N	E	S	S	E	E	Z	A

HAWAII (page 21)

M	A	U	N	A	L	O	A	I	U	A	M
A	K	S	S	A	A	V	A	L	A	O	J
U	A	H	H	O	N	O	L	U	L	U	A
N	U	E	A	F	A	O	A	O	U	T	T
A	A	L	W	R	I	S	K	Q	H	R	U
K	I	L	A	U	E	A	A	U	U	I	N
E	D	E	I	S	I	N	E	A	A	G	E
A	T	I	I	M	E	D	L	H	U	G	L
E	R	M	O	L	O	K	A	I	L	E	D
N	E	O	N	A	C	T	H	N	O	R	N
E	E	U	H	P	R	E	T	A	R	C	A
N	T	U	H	I	B	I	S	C	U	S	C

ILLINOIS (page 23)

Capitol
Chicago
Lincoln
Log Cabin
New Salem
Parks

KENTUCKY (page 27)

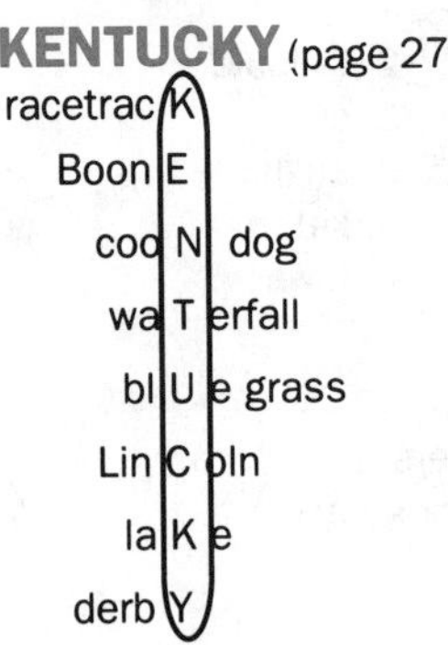

LOUISIANA (page 29)

face
falls
fan
feathers
feet
fence
fin
fingers
fish
flag
flamingo
flat tire
float
floodlight
flowers
footstool
fountain
fringe
frog
fruit

MICHIGAN (page 34)

HIKING
SKIING
SAILING
ROCK HUNTING
FISHING
SNOWMOBILING
CANOEING
SHOPPING
SWIMMING
CAMPING
HORSEBACK RIDING
MINE TOUR
MUSEUMS
PARKS
DUNES
WINDMILLS
FORTS
SOO LOCKS
ZOOS
BEACHES

MISSISSIPPI (page 36)

3	7	5
4	6	9
1	8	2

MISSOURI (page 37)

D	A	O	R	L	S	E	A	F	E	E	N	R	W
U	E	A	O	A	N	N	E	L	R	C	R	E	I
C	H	I	C	K	E	N	I	R	I	N	O	V	N
K	B	I	K	E	M	B	O	A	T	E	C	I	D
S	U	A	S	T	O	R	E	S	R	F	A	R	M
N	S	D	R	M	H	I	H	S	A	T	A	C	I
E	S	P	O	N	Y	D	I	P	N	P	A	I	L
D	L	T	O	W	N	G	O	U	P	E	P	N	L
R	U	A	O	A	N	E	O	G	Y	E	I	C	I
A	T	R	S	P	A	M	Y	A	W	H	G	I	H
G	O	L	F	C	O	U	R	S	E	S	S	P	O
O	L	I	S	R	A	T	R	A	C	T	O	R	R
N	A	E	C	O	W	B	E	A	C	H	I	P	S
S	S	R	E	W	O	L	F	O	R	E	S	T	E

MONTANA (page 38)

6. owlet — 2. tadpole
9. cygnet — 1. cub
10. gosling — 8. eaglet
3. kit — 5. kitten
7. lamb — 4. fawn

NEBRASKA (page 39)

Delaware, New Jersey
Mississippi, Minnesota
Florida, Missouri
Oregon, Michigan
Wisconsin, Nebraska
Tennessee, Arkansas
Iowa, Washington
Idaho, Maryland

NEVADA (page 40)

2. Cowboy hat — 6. Skis
8. Fish — 4. Golf club
5. Steam train — 3. Antique car
7. Power boat — 1. Gold

NORTH CAROLINA (pages 46-47)

Car into a Creature

CAR — CRATER
RACE — TERRACE
TRACE — CREATURE

Safety First

2 Merge
18 No Passing Zone
8 Do Not Enter
3 School Crossing
10 Slippery When Wet
14 Farm Machinery
4 No Right Turn
15 Cattle Crossing
5 Pedestrian Crossing
7 Stop
13 Road Curves
12 No U-Turn
9 Steep Hill
11 Yield
6 Deer Crossing
1 Railroad Crossing
17 Cross Road
16 No Bicycles

NORTH DAKOTA (page 48)

26 squares inside

OHIO (page 50)

Roller Coaster

OHIO HIGH FLYING

Computer Crazy

AN ECHO
BEANSTALK
A CANDLE
YOUR SHOE
A COIN
A COAT OF PAINT

OREGON (page 52)

Covered wagon — Kite
Crab — Rose
Grapes — Sand Castles

PENNSYLVANIA (pages 54-55)

7 Gettysburg — 2 Punxsutawney
6 Lancaster — 4 Scranton
5 Philadelphia — 1 Titusville
8 Pittsburgh — 3 Williamsport

TENNESSEE (pages 58-59)

Spectacular!

Grand Ole Opry
Nashville
Graceland
Memphis
Great Smoky Mountains
Chattanooga
Knoxville
Gatlinburg
Opryland

What's In a Name

1. Great Smoky Mountains National Park, NC and TN
2. The Badlands, North Dakota and South Dakota
3. Old Faithful geyser, Yellowstone National Park, Wyoming
4. Great Salt Lake, Utah
5. Oklahoma City, Oklahoma
6. Golden Gate Bridge, San Francisco, California
7. Mammoth Cave National Park, Kentucky
8. Maryland
9. Buffalo, New York
10. Little Rock, Arkansas
11. Bismarck, North Dakota
12. Washington, D.C.

UTAH (page 62)

CAPITOL REEF
ZION
RAINBOW BRIDGE
BRYCE CANYON
CANYONLANDS
ARCHES
DINOSAUR
CEDAR BREAKS

VIRGINIA (pages 64-65)

Discover America

1. Arizona, Colorado, New Mexico, Utah
2. Illinois, Indiana, Michigan, Wisconsin
3. Mississippi-Missouri River (3,740 miles)

4. Alaska (570,833 sq. mi.)
5. Rhode Island (1,054 sq. mi.)
6. Leadville, Colorado (10,152 ft.)
7. Yellowstone National Park (1872)
8. Mt. McKinley in Alaska (20,320 ft.)
9. Death Valley, California (-282 ft.)
10. Lake Superior
11. Philadelphia, Pennsylvania
12. San Francisco, California
13. South Dakota
14. Delaware (December 7, 1787)
15. Hawaii
16. Virginia

Who Was Who

WASHINGTON
MADISON
MONROE
WILSON
HARRISON
TYLER
TAYLOR
JEFFERSON

WEST VIRGINIA (page 67)

Kentucky — Maryland — Ohio
Virginia — Pennsylvania

WYOMING (page 69)

SKATES
SKIES
4 PAIRS OF MITTENS
WARM CLOTHES

CANADA (page 70)

BRITISH COLUMBIA
YUKON
PRINCE EDWARD ISLAND
MANITOBA
SASKATCHEWAN
ONTARIO
QUEBEC
NEWFOUNDLAND
NEW BRUNSWICK
NOVA SCOTIA
ALBERTA

INDEX TO COOL PLACES

Cities and towns in each state are listed in this Index. To find a city on a state map, find the city and its "map key" in the Index. Then turn to the map page and look for the city in the area identified by the "map key". For example, you will find Albertville in the B-4 area on the Alabama map.

ALABAMA
(Map on page 10)
Pop.: 4,062,600
Area: 50,766 Sq. Mi.

ALASKA
(Map on page 11)
Pop.: 551,900
Area: 570,833 Sq. Mi.

ARIZONA
(Map on page 12)
Pop.: 3,678,000
Area: 113,510 Sq. Mi.

ARKANSAS
(Map on page 13)
Pop.: 2,362,200
Area: 52,082 Sq. Mi.

CALIFORNIA
(Map on page 15)
Pop.: 29,839,300
Area: 156,297 Sq. Mi.

COLORADO
(Map on page 16)
Pop.: 3,307,900
Area: 103,598 Sq. Mi.

CONNECTICUT
(Map on page 17)
Pop.: 3,295,700
Area: 4,872 Sq. Mi.

DELAWARE
(Map on page 18)
Pop.: 668,700
Area: 1,933 Sq. Mi.

Wilmington B-10

DISTRICT OF COLUMBIA

(Map on page 9)
Pop.: 609,900
Area: 69 Sq. Mi.

FLORIDA

(Map on page 19)
Pop.: 13,003,400
Area: 54,157 Sq. Mi.

Arcadia E-3
Bartow D-3
Belle Glade F-5
Boca Raton F-5
Boynton Beach F-5
Bradenton E-3
Chattahoochee A-1,G-3
Clearwater D-3
Cocoa D-4
Coral Gables G-5
Crestview G-2
Daytona Beach C-4
DeLand C-4
Delray Beach F-5
Dunedin D-3
Ft. Lauderdale F-5
Ft. Meyers F-3
Ft. Pierce E-5
Ft. Walton Beach G-2
Gainesville B-3
Hialeah F-5
Hollywood F-5
Jacksonville B-4
Jacksonville Beach B-4
Key West H-3
Lake City B-3
Lakeland D-3
Lake Wales D-4
Lake Worth F-5
Leesburg C-3
Marathon H-4
Melbourne D-5
Miami G-5
Miami Beach G-5
Naples F-4
Ocala C-3
Orlando C-4
Ormond Beach C-4
Palatka B-4
Panama City H-3
Pensacola G-1
Perry B-2
Plant City D-3
Pompano Beach F-5
Riviera Beach E-5
St. Augustine B-4
St. Petersburg D-3
Sanford C-4
Sarasota E-3
Sebring E-4
Tallahassee A-1
Tampa D-3
Titusville C-4
Venice E-3
Vero Beach D-5
W. Palm Beach E-5
W. Pensacola G-1
Winter Haven D-4
Winter Park C-4

GEORGIA

(Map on page 20)
Pop.: 6,508,400
Area: 58,060 Sq. Mi.

Albany F-2
Americus E-2
Athens C-3
Atlanta C-2
Augusta D-4
Bainbridge G-2
Baxley F-4
Blakely F-1
Brunswick F-5
Cairo G-2
Carollton D-1
Clayton B-3
Columbus E-1
Cordele E-2
Covington D-2
Dahlonega B-2
Dalton B-1
Decator C-2
Dublin E-3
Fitzgerald F-3
Gainesville C-2
Griffin D-2
Jesup F-4
La Grange D-1
Macon D-3
McRae E-3
Marietta C-2
Milledgeville D-3
Monroe C-2
Moultrie F-2
Newnan D-1
Perry E-2
Rome C-1
Savannah E-5
Statesboro E-4
Thomasville G-2
Tifton F-3
Valdosta G-3
Warner Robins E-3
Waycross F-4
Waynesboro D-4

HAWAII

(Map on page 21)
Pop.: 1,115,300
Area: 6,427 Sq. Mi.

Hilo G-5
Honolulu F-2,F-3
Kahana G-2
Kahului F-4
Kailua F-3,H-3
Kaneohe F-3,G-3
Kapaa E-2
Kawela F-2
Lahaina F-4
Nanakuli G-1
Pearl City F-3,H-2
Puuanahulu G-4
Puunene F-4
Wahiawa F-3,G-2
Wailuku F-4

IDAHO

(Map on page 22)
Pop.: 1,012,000
Area: 82,413 Sq. Mi.

American Falls G-4
Blackfoot G-4
Boise F-1
Bonners Ferry A-1
Burley H-3
Caldwell F-1
Coeur d'Alene B-1
Grangeville D-1
Idaho Falls F-4
Jerome G-3
Kellogg B-2
Lewiston C-1
Montpelier H-5
Moscow C-1
Nampa F-1
Payette F-1
Pocatello G-4
Preston H-5
Rexburg F-5
St. Anthony F-5
Shelley G-4
Sun Valley F-3
Twin Falls G-3
Weiser F-1

ILLINOIS

(Map on page 23)
Pop.: 11,466,700
Area: 55,646 Sq. Mi.

Alton F-2
Arlington Hts. A-4
Aurora B-4
Belleville F-2
Belvidere A-4
Bloomington D-3
Cairo H-3
Carbondale G-3
Carmi G-4
Centralia F-3
Champaign D-4
Charleston E-4
Chicago A-5
Chicago Heights B-5
Collinsville F-2
Danville D-5
Decatur D-4
De Kalb A-4
Dixon B-3
East St. Louis F-2
Effingham E-4
Elgin A-4
Evanston A-5
Freeport A-3
Galena A-2
Galesburg C-2
Harrisburg G-4
Highland Park A-5
Jacksonville E-2
Joliet B-4
Kankakee C-5
Kewanee B-3
Lincoln D-3
Macomb D-2
Marion G-4
Marshall E-5
Mattoon E-4
Moline B-2
Monmouth C-2
Mt. Carmel F-5
Mt. Vernon G-4
Nauvoo C-1
Newton F-4
Normal C-3
Ottawa B-4
Pekin C-3
Peoria C-3
Peru B-3
Pittsfield E-2
Pontiac C-4
Quincy D-1
Rantoul D-4
Rock Falls B-3
Rockford A-3
Rock Island B-2
Springfield D-3
Sterling B-3
Streator C-4
Urbana D-4
Vandalia F-3
Watseka C-5
Waukegan A-5
W. Frankfort G-4
Woodstock A-4

INDIANA

(Map on page 24)
Pop.: 5,564,200
Area: 35,936 Sq. Mi.

Anderson D-4
Angola A-5
Bedford F-3
Bloomington F-3
Brazil E-2
Clinton E-2
Columbus F-4
Connersville E-5
Crawfordsville D-2
Crown Point A-2
Decatur B-5
Elkhart A-4
Elwood D-4
Evansville H-1
Fort Wayne B-5
Frankfort D-3
Franklin E-4
French Lick G-3
Gary A-2
Goshen A-4
Greencastle E-2
Greenfield D-4
Griffith A-2
Hartford City C-5
Huntington B-4
Indianapolis E-3
Kokomo C-3
Lafayette C-2
La Porte A-3
Lebanon D-3
Logansport C-3
Madison F-5
Marion C-4
Martinsville E-3
Michigan City A-2
Mishawaka A-3
Muncie D-4
New Albany G-4
New Castle D-5
Noblesville D-4
Peru C-4
Plymouth A-3
Portage A-2
Portland C-5
Princeton G-1
Richmond D-5
Rockport H-2
Rockville E-2
Scottsburg G-4
Seymour F-4
Shelbyville E-4
South Bend A-3
Terre Haute E-2
Valparaiso A-2
Versailles F-5
Wabash C-4
Warsaw B-4
Washington G-2
W. Lafayette C-2

IOWA

(Map on page 25)
Pop.: 2,787,400
Area: 55,965 Sq. Mi.

Ames C-4
Atlantic D-3
Burlington E-7
Cedar Falls B-6
Cedar Rapids C-6
Centerville E-5
Charles City A-5
Cherokee B-2
Clinton C-8
Council Bluffs D-2
Creston D-3
Davenport D-8
Decorah A-6
Des Moines D-4
Dubuque B-8
Estherville A-3
Fairfield D-6
Ft. Dodge B-4
Ft. Madison E-7
Grinnell C-5
Iowa City C-7
Knoxville D-5
Le Mars B-1
Marshalltown C-5
Mason City A-5
Muscatine D-7
Newton C-5
Oelwein B-6
Oskaloosa D-5
Ottumwa D-6
Red Oak D-2
Rock Rapids A-1
Shenandoah E-2
Sioux City B-1
Spencer A-2
Storm Lake B-2
Washington D-6
Waterloo B-6
Webster City B-4

KANSAS

(Map on page 28)
Pop.: 2,485,600
Area: 81,783 Sq. Mi.

Abilene C-6
Atchison B-8
Belleville A-5
Chanute D-7
Colby B-2
Concordia B-5
Dodge City D-3
El Dorado D-6
Emporia C-7
Ft. Scott D-8
Garden City D-2
Goodland B-1
Great Bend C-4
Hays C-3
Hutchinson D-5
Independence E-7
Junction City B-6
Kansas City B-8
Lawrence B-8
Leavenworth B-8
Liberal E-2
McPherson C-5
Manhattan B-6
Marysville A-6
Oakley B-2
Olathe C-8
Ottawa C-8
Parsons D-8
Phillipsburg B-3
Pittsburg D-8
Pratt D-4
St. Francis A-1
Salina C-5
Syracuse D-1
Topeka B-7
Tribune C-1
Wellington E-5
Wichita D-5
Winfield E-6

KENTUCKY

(Map on page 26-27)
Pop.: 3,699,000
Area: 39,674 Sq. Mi.

Ashland B-9
Barbourville E-8
Bardstown C-6
Beaver Dam D-4
Berea D-7
Bowling Green E-5
Columbia D-6
Corbin E-8
Covington B-7
Cumberland E-9
Danville D-7
Elizabethtown D-6
Frankfort C-7
Fulton E-2
Glasgow E-6
Harrodsburg C-7
Hazard D-9

Henderson C-4
Hodgenville D-6
Hopkinsville E-4
Lawrenceburg C-7
Lexington C-7
Louisville C-6
Madisonville D-4
Mayfield E-3
Maysville B-8
Middlesboro E-8
Morehead C-8
Morgantown D-5
Murray E-3
Newport B-7
Owensboro C-4
Paducah D-3
Paris C-7
Pikeville D-9
Pineville E-8
Prestonsburg D-9
Richmond C-7
Salyersville C-9
Somerset D-7

LOUISIANA

(Map on page 29)
Pop.: 4,238,200
Area: 44,520 Sq. Mi.

Abbeville J-4
Alexandria G-3
Baton Rouge H-5
Bogalusa H-6
Bossier City F-2
Chalmette J-6
Crowley J-4
Eunice H-4
Hammond H-6
Jennings J-3
Lafayette J-4
Lake Charles J-2
Metairie J-6
Monroe F-4
Morgan City J-5
Natchitoches G-3
New Iberia J-4
New Orleans J-6
Opelousas H-4
Port Sulphur K-7
Ruston F-3
Shreveport F-2
Sulphur J-2
Tallulah F-5
Winnfield G-3

MAINE

(Map on page 30)
Pop.: 1,233,200
Area: 30,995 Sq. Mi.

Auburn F-2
Augusta F-2
Bangor E-3
Biddeford G-1
Brewer E-3
Brunswick G-2
Caribou B-4
Eastport E-5
Ellsworth F-4
Fort Kent A-3
Gardiner F-2
Houlton C-4
Jackman D-2
Lewiston F-2
Madawaska A-4
Mattawamkeag D-4
Pittsfield E-3
Portland G-2
Presque Isle B-4
Rangeley E-1
Rockland F-3
Saco G-1
Skowhegan E-2
Waterville F-2
Westbrook G-1

MARYLAND

(Map on page 31)
Pop.: 4,798,600
Area: 9,838 Sq. Mi.

Aberdeen C-9
Annapolis C-9
Baltimore C-9
Bel Air C-9
Cambridge D-9
Cumberland C-6
Easton D-9
Frederick C-8
Frostburg C-6
Hagerstown C-7
La Plata D-8
Lexington Park D-9
Oakland C-6
Ocean City D-10
Pocomoke
City E-10
Reisterstown C-8
Rockville C-8
Salisbury D-10
Westminster C-8

MASSACHUSETTS

(Map on page 32-33)
Pop.: 6,029,100
Area: 7,826 Sq. Mi.

Adams B-2
Athol B-4
Attleboro E-7
Boston C-7
Brockton D-8
Cambridge C-7
Chicopee D-3
Edgartown F-9
Fall River E-7
Fitchburg B-6
Framingham C-7
Gardner B-5
Gloucester B-8
Grafton D-6
Greenfield B-3
Haverhill B-7
Holyoke D-3
Hyannis F-9
Lawrence B-7
Leominster C-6
Lexington C-7
Lowell B-7
Lynn C-8
Marlborough C-6
Milford D-6
New Bedford F-8
N. Adams B-2
Northampton C-3
Pittsfield C-2
Provincetown D-10
Quincy D-8
Southbridge D-5
Springfield D-4
Webster D-5
Westfield D-3
Weymouth D-8
Woburn C-7
Worcester C-6

MICHIGAN

(Map on page 34)
Pop.: 9,328,800
Area: 56,959 Sq. Mi.

Albion G-3
Alpena D-4
Ann Arbor G-4
Battle Creek G-3
Bay City E-4
Benton Harbor G-2
Birmingham G-5
Cadillac E-3
Dearborn G-5
Detroit G-5
Escanaba C-1
Flint F-4
Grand Haven F-2
Grand Rapids F-2
Hillsdale H-3
Holland F-2
Iron Mountain B-5
Ishpeming B-1
Jackson G-4
Kalamazoo G-2
Lansing G-3
Livonia G-4
Ludington E-2
Mackinaw City C-3
Marquette B-1
Menominee C-1
Midland E-4
Monroe H-4
Mount
Clemens G-5
Muskegon F-2
Niles H-2
Owosso F-4
Pontiac G-5
Portage G-2
Port Huron F-5
Saginaw F-4
Sault Ste.
Marie B-4
Three Rivers H-2
Traverse City D-2
Trenton G-5
Ypsilanti G-4

MINNESOTA

(Map on page 35)
Pop.: 4,387,000
Area: 79,548 Sq. Mi.

Albert Lea H-4
Alexandria E-2
Austin H-4
Bemidji C-2
Bloomington F-4
Brainerd E-3
Cambridge F-4
Chisholm C-4
Cloquet D-4
Crookston C-1
Duluth D-5
E. Grand Forks C-1
Ely C-5
Fairmont H-3
Faribault G-4
Fergus Falls E-1
Hibbing C-4
Hutchinson F-3
International
Falls B-3
Mankato G-3
Marshall G-2
Minneapolis F-4
Moorhead D-1
New Ulm G-3
Northfield G-4
Owatonna H-4
Pine City E-4
Rochester G-4
Roseau B-2
St. Cloud F-3
St. Paul F-4
St. Peter G-3
Sandstone E-4
Thief River
Falls C-1
Virginia C-4
White Bear
Lake F-4
Willmar F-2
Winona G-5
Worthington H-2

MISSISSIPPI

(Map on page 36)
Pop.: 2,586,400
Area: 47,234 Sq. Mi.

Aberdeen D-8
Biloxi H-8
Booneville C-8
Brookhaven G-6
Canton F-6
Clarksdale D-6
Cleveland D-5
Columbia G-6
Columbus D-8
Corinth C-8
Greenville E-5
Greenwood D-6
Grenada D-6
Gulfport H-7
Hattiesburg G-7
Holly Sprs. C-7
Indianola D-5
Jackson F-6
Kosciusko E-7
Laurel G-7
Louisville E-7
McComb G-6
Mendenhall F-6
Meridian F-8
Moss Pt. H-8
Natchez G-5
New Albany C-7
Oxford C-7
Pascagoula H-8
Philadelphia E-7
Quitman F-8
Senatobia C-6
Starkville D-7
Tupelo C-8
Vicksburg F-5
Winona D-7
Woodville H-5
Yazoo City E-6

MISSOURI

(Map on page 37)
Pop.: 5,137,800
Area: 68,945 Sq. Mi.

Bethany A-3
Boonville B-4
Cape
Girardeau D-7
Carthage D-3
Chillicothe B-4
Columbia B-5
Eldon C-4
Excelsior
Springs B-3
Festus C-6
Fulton C-5
Hannibal B-5
Independence B-3
Jefferson City C-5
Joplin D-3
Kansas City B-3
Kennett E-6
Kirksville A-4
Lees Summit B-3
Marshall B-4
Mexico B-5
Milan A-4
Moberly B-4
Mound City A-2
Nevada D-3
New Madrid E-7
Palmyra B-5
Piedmont D-6
Poplar Bluff E-6
Rolla C-5
St. Charles C-6
St. Joseph B-3
St. Louis C-6
Salem D-5
Sedalia C-4
Sikeston D-7
Springfield D-4
Warrensburg C-3
W. Plains E-5

MONTANA

(Map on page 38)
Pop.: 803,700
Area: 145,388 Sq. Mi.

Anaconda D-3
Billings D-5
Bozeman D-4
Browning A-3
Butte D-3
Columbia Falls A-2
Deer Lodge C-3
Dillon D-3
Ekalaka D-8
Eureka A-1
Glasgow B-7
Glendive C-8
Great Falls B-4
Hardin D-6
Harlem A-5
Havre A-5
Helena C-3
Kalispell B-2
Lewistown C-5
Libby A-1
Livingston D-4
Miles City C-7
Missoula C-2
Philipsburg C-2
Roundup C-5
Shelby A-3
Superior C-1
Thompson
Falls B-1
Whitefish A-2
Wolf Pt. B-7

NEBRASKA

(Map on page 39)
Pop.: 1,584,600
Area: 76,639 Sq. Mi.

Ainsworth B-4
Alliance B-2
Alma E-5
Auburn D-8
Bayard C-1
Beatrice D-7
Blair C-8
Bridgeport C-1
Broken Bow C-4
Crawford A-1
Fairbury D-7
Falls City D-8
Fremont C-7
Gering B-1
Grand Island D-6
Hastings D-6
Holdrege D-5
Kimball C-1
Lincoln D-7
Loup City C-5
McCook D-4
Nebraska City D-8
Neligh B-6
Norfolk B-6
North Platte C-4
Ogallala C-3
Omaha C-8
O'Neill B-5
Oshkosh C-2
Plattsmouth C-8
Red Cloud D-6
Rushville A-2
Scottsbluff B-1
Seward D-7
Sidney C-2
Syracuse D-8
Valentine A-4
Wayne B-7
York D-6

NEVADA
(Map on page 40)
Pop.: 1,206,200
Area: 109,895 Sq. Mi.

Austin C-6
Babbitt D-5
Battle Mtn. B-6
Boulder City G-8
Carlin B-7
Carson City D-4
Elko B-7
Ely C-8
Empire B-4
Eureka C-7
Fallon C-5
Hawthorne D-5
Henderson G-8
Indian Sprs. F-7
Las Vegas G-8
Lovelock C-5
N. Las Vegas G-8
Reno C-4
Sparks C-4
Tonopah E-6
Warm Sprs. D-7
Wells B-7
Winnemucca B-5
Yerington D-4

NEW HAMPSHIRE
(Map on page 41)
Pop.: 1,113,900
Area: 8,992 Sq. Mi.

Ashland E-4
Berlin C-4
Bristol E-4
Center Ossipee E-5
Claremont F-3
Colebrook B-4
Concord F-4
Conway D-5
Derry G-4
Dover F-5
Franklin E-4
Hampton G-5
Keene G-3
Laconia E-4
Lebanon E-3
Littleton C-3
Manchester G-4
Nashua G-4
N. Woodstock D-4
Peterborough G-3
Portsmouth F-5
Rochester F-5
Salem G-4
Winchester G-3
Woodsville D-3

NEW JERSEY
(Map on page 42)
Pop.: 7,748,600
Area: 7,468 Sq. Mi.

Asbury Park D-5
Atlantic City G-3
Bayonne C-4
Bloomfield B-4
Bridgeton G-2
Burlington E-3
Camden E-2
Clifton B-4
Denville B-3
Eatontown D-4
Elizabeth C-4
Freehold D-4
Glassboro F-2
Hamburg A-3
Hammonton F-3
Jersey City C-4
Lakewood E-4
Linden C-4
Long Branch D-5
Millville G-2
Morristown B-3
Newark B-4
New Brunswick C-3
Newton B-3
Oakland B-4
Paterson B-4
Perth Amboy C-4
Phillipsburg C-2
Plainfield C-3
Pleasantville G-3
Pt. Pleasant E-4
Princeton D-3
Red Bank D-4
Salem F-1
Somerville C-3
Trenton D-3
Vineland G-2
Washington C-2
Willingboro E-2

NEW MEXICO
(Map on page 43)
Pop.: 1,521,800
Area: 121,336 Sq. Mi.

Alamogordo F-8
Albuquerque D-7
Artesia F-9
Belen D-7
Carlsbad F-9
Clovis E-10
Deming G-7
Espanola C-8
Farmington B-6
Gallup D-6
Grants D-6
Hobbs F-10
Las Cruces G-7
Las Vegas C-8
Los Alamos C-8
Lovington F-10
Portales E-10
Raton B-9
Roswell F-9
Santa Fe C-8
Silver City F-6
Socorro E-7
Truth or Consequences F-7
Tucumcari D-10
University Park G-7

NEW YORK
(Map on page 44-45)
Pop.: 18,044,500
Area: 47,379 Sq. Mi.

Albany E-9
Amsterdam E-9
Auburn E-5
Batavia E-3
Bay Shore H-3
Beacon G-9
Binghamton F-6
Buffalo E-2
Cheektowaga E-2
Cooperstown E-8
Corning F-5
Cortland E-6
Depew E-2
Dunkirk F-1
Eastport H-4
Elmira F-5
Freeport H-2
Fulton D-6
Geneva E-5
Gloversville D-9
Hampton Bays H-4
Hornell F-4
Huntington H-3
Ithaca F-6
Jamestown F-2
Jericho H-2
Kingston G-9
Lackawanna E-2
Lockport D-2
Massena A-8
Merrick H-2
Middletown H-9
Mt Vernon G-2
Newburgh G-9
New Rochelle G-2
New York H-1
Niagara Falls D-2
Ogdensburg A-7
Olean F-3
Oneonta F-8
Ossining H-9
Oswego D-6
Patchogue H-3
Peekskill H-9
Plattsburgh A-10
Port Jefferson G-3
Potsdam A-8
Poughkeepsie G-9
Riverhead G-4
Rochester D-4
Rome D-7
Saratoga Springs D-9
Schenectady E-9
Smithtown H-3
Southampton G-5
Syracuse D-6
Troy E-10
Utica D-7
Watertown C-6
White Plains G-2,H-10

NORTH CAROLINA
(Map on page 46-47)
Pop.: 6,657,600
Area: 48,843 Sq. Mi.

Albemarle C-5
Asheville C-3
Burlington B-6
Charlotte C-4
Cherokee C-2
Concord C-5
Durham B-7
Elizabeth City B-9
Elizabethtown D-7
Fayetteville D-7
Gastonia C-4
Goldsboro C-8
Greensboro B-6
Greenville C-8
Havelock D-9
Hickory C-4
High Point B-5
Jacksonville D-8
Kannapolis C-5
Kinston C-8
Kitty Hawk B-10
Laurinburg D-6
Lenoir C-4
Lumberton D-7
Manteo B-10
Monroe D-5
Morganton C-3
Mt. Airy B-5
New Bern D-9
Raleigh C-7
Rocky Mt. B-8
Salisbury C-5
Sanford C-6
Tarboro B-8
Thomasville C-5
Washington C-9
Wilmington E-8
Wilson C-8
Winston-Salem B-5

NORTH DAKOTA
(Map on page 48)
Pop.: 641,400
Area: 69,299 Sq. Mi.

Belfield D-2
Bismarck D-4
Bottineau A-4
Bowbells A-3
Bowman E-1
Carrington C-6
Casselton D-7
Edgeley E-6
Ellendale E-6
Fargo D-8
Grand Forks B-7
Harvey C-5
Jamestown D-6
Kenmare B-3
Killdeer C-2
Mandan D-4
Northwood C-7
Oakes E-7
Pembina A-7
Stanley B-2
Tioga B-2
Velva B-4
Wahpeton E-8
Walhalla A-7
Williston B-1

OHIO
(Map on page 51)
Pop.: 10,887,300
Area: 41,004 Sq. Mi.

Akron D-7
Alliance D-7
Ashland D-5
Ashtabula B-8
Athens H-6
Bellefontaine E-3
Bowling Green C-3
Cambridge F-7
Canton D-7
Chillicothe H-4
Cincinnati H-1
Circleville G-4
Cleveland C-6
Columbus G-4
Coshocton F-6
Cuyahoga Falls D-7
Dayton G-2
Defiance C-1
Delaware F-4
Elyria C-6
Euclid C-7
Findlay D-3
Fostoria D-3
Fremont C-4
Gallipolis J-5
Greenville F-1
Hamilton H-1
Ironton K-5
Kettering G-2
Lakewood C-6
Lancaster G-5
Lima D-2
Lorain C-5
Mansfield D-5
Marietta H-7
Marion E-4
Martins Fy. F-8
Massillon D-7
Middletown G-1
Mt. Vernon E-5
Newark F-5
Norwalk C-5
Norwood H-1
Painesville B-7
Parma C-6
Portsmouth J-4
Ravenna D-7
Salem D-8
Sandusky C-4
Shaker Hts. C-7
Springfield G-2
Steubenville E-8
Toledo B-3
Troy F-2
Van Wert D-1
Warren C-8
Washington C.H. G-3
Wilmington H-2
Wooster D-6
Youngstown D-8
Zanesville G-6

OKLAHOMA
(Map on page 49)
Pop.: 3,157,600
Area: 68,656 Sq. Mi.

Ada C-6
Altus C-4
Alva A-5
Anadarko C-5
Ardmore D-6
Atoka D-7
Bartlesville A-7
Blackwell A-6
Boise City A-1
Chickasha C-5
Clinton B-4
Cushing B-6
Duncan C-5
Durant D-7
Elk City B-4
Enid A-5
Guthrie B-6
Guymon A-2
Henryetta B-7
Hugo D-7
Idabel D-8
Lawton C-5
McAlester C-7
Miami A-8
Midwest City B-6
Muskogee B-7
Norman C-6
Oklahoma City B-6
Okmulgee B-7
Ponca City A-6
Sapulpa B-7
Seminole C-6
Shawnee C-6
Stillwater B-6
Tulsa B-7
Waynoka A-4
Weatherford B-4
Woodward A-4

OREGON
(Map on page 52)
Pop.: 2,853,700
Area: 96,187 Sq. Mi.

Albany B-3
Ashland E-3
Astoria A-2
Baker B-7
Bend C-4
Brookings E-2
Burns D-6
Condon B-5
Coos Bay D-2
Corvallis C-2
Dallas B-2
Enterprise B-7
Eugene C-3
Florence C-2
Forest Grove B-3
Gold Beach E-1
Grants Pass E-2
Hillsboro B-3

Jordan Valley D-7
Klamath Falls E-4
La Grande B-6
Lakeview E-5
La Pine D-4
Medford E-3
Milton-Freewater A-6
Newport B-2
North Bend D-2
Nyssa C-7
Ontario C-7
Oregon City B-3
Pendleton A-6
Portland B-3
Port Orford D-1
Redmond C-4
Roseburg D-2
Salem B-3
Silver Lake D-4
Springfield C-3
The Dalles B-4

PENNSYLVANIA

(Map on page 54-55)
Pop.: 11,924,700
Area: 44,892 Sq. Mi.

Allentown E-9
Altoona F-4
Beaver Falls E-1
Bedford G-4
Berwick D-8
Bethlehem E-9
Bloomsburg D-7
Canonsburg F-1
Carbondale C-9
Carlisle F-6
Chambersburg G-5
Chester G-9
Clairton F-2
Clarion D-3
Coatesville G-8
Connellsville G-2
Du Bois D-4
Easton E-9
E. Stroudsburg D-10
Erie B-1
Franklin C-2
Gettysburg G-6
Glenshaw E-2
Greensburg F-2
Hanover G-7
Harrisburg F-7
Hazleton E-8
Indiana E-3
Johnstown F-3
Kingston D-8
Kittanning E-2
Lancaster G-8
Lebanon F-8
Lewistown E-6
McKeesport F-2
Mansfield C-6
Meadville C-1
Milford D-10
Mt. Carmel E-8
New Castle D-1
Norristown F-9
Oil City C-2
Philadelphia G-10
Pittsburgh F-2
Pittston D-8
Port Allegany C-4
Pottstown F-9
Pottsville E-8
Reading F-8
Ridgway C-4
Scranton C-9
Sharon D-1
State College E-5
Sunbury E-7
Titusville C-2
Towanda C-7
Uniontown G-2
Upper Darby G-9
Warren C-3
Washington F-1
Waynesboro G-6
Wilkes-Barre D-8
Wilkinsburg F-2
Williamsport D-7
York G-7

RHODE ISLAND

(Map on page 53)
Pop.: 1,006,000
Area: 1,054 Sq. Mi.

Bristol F-7
Cranston E-7
Kingston F-6
Middletown F-7
Newport F-7
Pawtucket E-7
Providence E-7
Wakefield F-6
Warwick E-7
Westerly G-6
Woonsocket D-6

SOUTH CAROLINA

(Map on page 56)
Pop.: 3,505,700
Area: 30,207 Sq. Mi.

Aiken F-3
Allendale G-4
Anderson D-2
Andrews F-6
Bamberg F-4
Batesburg E-4
Beaufort G-5
Bennettsville D-6
Charleston G-5
Clemson D-2
Clinton E-3
Columbia E-4
Conway E-7
Darlington E-6
Dillon E-6
Easley D-3
Florence E-6
Gaffney D-4
Georgetown F-6
Greenville D-3
Greer D-3
Hartsville E-5
Kingstree F-6
Lake City E-6
Lancaster D-4
Laurens D-3
Myrtle Beach F-7
North Augusta F-3
N. Charleston G-5
Orangeburg F-4
Ridgeland G-4
Rock Hill D-4
Spartanburg D-3
Summerville F-5
Sumter E-5
Union D-4
Walterboro G-5
Whitmire D-4

SOUTH DAKOTA

(Map on page 57)
Pop.: 700,000
Area: 75,956 Sq. Mi.

Aberdeen A-6
Arlington C-7
Armour D-6
Belle Fourche B-1
Brookings C-8
Custer D-1
Faith B-3
Gettysburg B-5
Hot Springs D-1
Lemmon A-3
Madison C-8
Mitchell D-7
Mobridge A-4
Philip C-3
Pierre C-4
Plankinton D-6
Presho C-5
Rapid City C-2
Redfield B-6
Sioux Falls D-8
Sisseton A-8
Spearfish C-1
Sturgis C-1
Watertown B-8
Yankton E-7

TENNESSEE

(Map on page 58-59)
Pop.: 4,896,600
Area: 41,154 Sq. Mi.

Athens G-7
Bolivar G-2
Bristol E-10
Chattanooga G-6
Clarksville E-4
Cleveland G-7
Columbia F-4
Cookeville F-6
Crossville F-7
Dyersburg F-2
Elizabethton E-10
Fayetteville G-5
Greeneville F-9
Harriman F-7
Henderson G-2
Hohenwald G-4
Humbolt F-2
Jackson F-2
Johnson City E-10
Kingsport E-9
Knoxville F-8
Lafayette E-5
Lawrenceburg G-4
Lebanon F-5
McMinnville F-6
Maryville F-8
Memphis G-1
Millington G-1
Morristown F-9
Murfreesboro F-5
Nashville F-5
Oak Ridge F-7
Paris E-3
Ripley F-2
Rogersville E-9
Shelbyville G-5
Soddy-Daisy G-7
Tullahoma G-5
Union City E-2
Waverly F-3

TEXAS

(Map on page 60-61)
Pop.: 17,059,800
Area: 262,015 Sq. Mi.

Abilene B-6
Amarillo A-4
Arlington B-8
Austin D-7
Baytown D-9
Beaumont D-10
Big Spring B-4
Borger A-5
Brownfield B-4
Brownsville H-7
Brownwood C-6
Bryan D-8
Corpus Christi F-7
Corsicana B-8
Dallas B-8
Del Rio E-5
Denton B-8
Eagle Pass E-5
El Paso C-1
Ft. Worth B-7
Freeport E-9
Gainesville A-7
Galveston E-9
Harlingen H-7
Houston D-9
Huntsville D-9
Jacksonville C-9
Kermit C-3
Kerrville D-6
Kingsville F-7
Lake Jackson E-9
Lamesa B-4
Laredo F-6
Longview B-9
Lubbock A-4
Lufkin C-9
McAllen G-7
Marshall B-9
Midland C-4
Nacogdoches C-9
Odessa C-4
Orange D-10
Palestine C-9
Paris A-9
Pecos C-3
Perryton A-5
Plainview A-4
Port Arthur D-10
Presidio E-2
Raymondville G-7
San Angelo C-5
San Antonio E-7
San Marcos D-7
Sherman A-8
Snyder B-5
Sulphur Springs B-9
Sweetwater B-5
Temple C-7
Texarkana A-10
Texas City E-9
Tyler B-9
Vernon A-6
Victoria E-8
Waco C-8
Waxahachie B-8
Wichita Falls A-7

UTAH

(Map on page 62)
Pop.: 1,727,800
Area: 82,076 Sq. Mi.

American Fork C-3
Bountiful C-3
Brigham City B-3
Cedar City G-2
Clearfield B-3
Green River E-4
Kearns C-3
Layton C-3
Loa F-3
Logan B-3
Moab F-5
Murray C-3
Ogden B-3
Orem C-3
Price D-4
Provo D-3
Richfield E-3
St. George G-1
Salt Lake City C-3
Smithfield B-3
Spanish Fork D-3
Tremonton B-2
Vernal C-5
Vernon D-2
Wendover C-1

VERMONT

(Map on page 63)
Pop.: 565,000
Area: 9,273 Sq. Mi.

Barre D-2
Bennington G-1
Bradford D-3
Brattleboro G-2
Burlington C-1
Fair Haven E-1
Island Pond B-3
Lyndonville C-3
Manchester F-1
Middlebury D-1
Montpelier D-2
Newport B-3
Northfield D-2
Norton B-3
Poultney E-1
Rutland E-1
St. Albans B-1
St. Johnsbury C-3
Springfield F-2
Swanton B-1
Waterbury C-2
Winooski C-1
Woodstock E-2

VIRGINIA

(Map on page 64-65)
Pop.: 6,216,600
Area: 39,700 Sq. Mi.

Alexandria D-8
Arlington D-8
Big Stone Gap F-2
Bowling Green E-8
Bristol G-2
Buena Vista E-6
Charlottesville E-7
Chesapeake G-9
Colonial Hts. F-8
Covington E-5
Danville G-6
Emporia G-8
Franklin G-8
Fredricksburg D-8
Front Royal D-7
Hampton F-9
Harrisonburg D-6
Lynchburg F-6
Martinsville G-5
New Market D-6
Newport News F-9
Norfolk F-9
Onancock E-10
Orange E-7
Petersburg F-8
Portsmouth G-9
Pulaski F-4
Radford F-4
Reedville E-9
Richmond F-8
Roanoke F-5
Staunton E-6
Suffolk G-9
Tappahannock E-8
Tazewell F-3
Virginia Beach F-9
Warrenton D-7
Waynesboro E-6
Williamsburg F-9
Winchester C-7
Wytheville F-4

WASHINGTON
(Map on page 66)
Pop.: 4,887,900
Area: 66,512 Sq. Mi.

Aberdeen C-2
Auburn C-3
Bellevue C-3
Bellingham A-3
Blaine A-3
Bremerton C-3
Camas E-3
Clarkston D-8
Colville A-7
Coulee City C-6
Ellensburg C-5
Ephrata C-6
Everett B-3
Hoquiam C-2
Kennewick D-6
Longview D-2
Moses Lake C-6
Mt. Vernon B-3
Olympia C-3
Omak B-6
Oroville A-6
Parkland C-3
Pasco D-6
Port Angeles B-2
Pullman D-8
Renton C-3
Richland D-6
Seattle C-3
Sedro Woolley A-3
Spokane C-8
Sunnyside D-5
Tacoma C-3
Toppenish D-5
Vancouver E-3
Walla Walla E-7
Wenatchee C-5
White Salmon E-4
Yakima D-5

WEST VIRGINIA
(Map on page 67)
Pop.: 1,801,600
Area: 24,124 Sq. Mi.

Beckley E-4
Bluefield F-3
Charleston D-3
Clarksburg C-4
Elkins D-5
Fairmont C-5
Franklin D-6
Huntington D-2
Logan E-3
Madison E-3
Marlinton E-5
Martinsburg C-7
Morgantown C-5
New Martinsville C-4
Parkersburg C-3
Petersburg D-6
Pt. Pleasant D-3
Princeton F-4
Spencer D-3
Summersville E-4
Weirton B-4
Weston C-4
Wheeling B-4
White Sulphur Springs E-4

WISCONSIN
(Map on page 68)
Pop.: 4,906,700
Area: 54,424 Sq. Mi.

Appleton E-4
Ashland C-2
Baraboo F-3
Beaver Dam G-4
Beloit G-4
Chippewa Falls E-2
Eagle River D-3
Eau Claire E-2
Fond du Lac F-4
Green Bay E-4
Hayward C-2
Janesville G-4
Kenosha G-5
La Crosse F-2
Lake Geneva G-4
Madison G-3
Manitowoc F-5
Marinette D-5
Marshfield E-3
Menomonee Falls G-4
Merrill D-3
Milwaukee G-5
Neenah F-4
Oshkosh F-4
Prairie du Chien G-2
Racine G-5
Rhinelander D-3
Rice Lake D-2
Shawano E-4
Sheboygan F-5
Stevens Pt. E-3
Sturgeon Bay E-5
Superior C-1
Two Rivers F-5
Waukesha G-4
Wausau E-3
Wisconsin Dells F-3
Wisconsin Rapids E-3

WYOMING
(Map on page 69)
Pop.: 456,000
Area: 96,988 Sq. Mi.

Buffalo A-5
Casper C-6
Cheyenne E-7
Cody A-3
Douglas C-6
Evanston E-2
Gillette B-6
Green River E-3
Jackson B-2
Lander C-4
Laramie E-6
Lovell A-4
Lusk C-7
Mammoth Hot Springs A-2
Newcastle B-7
Pinedale C-3
Powell A-3
Rawlins D-5
Riverton C-4
Rock Sprs. E-3
Sheridan A-5
Sundance A-7
Thermopolis B-4
Torrington D-7
Worland B-4

CANADA
(Map on page 70-71)
Pop.: 24,343,181
Area: 3,851,809 Sq. Mi.

Brandon G-4
Calgary G-3
Campbell River F-1
Chicoutimi G-8
Corner Brook F-10
Dawson C-1
Dawson Creek F-2
Edmonton F-3
Flin Flon F-4
Fort McMurray F-3
Fredericton G-9
Halifax G-9
Hamilton H-7
Kamloops G-2
Kapuskasing G-7
Kenora G-5
Kitchener H-7
Lethbridge G-3
London H-7
Medicine Hat G-3
Montréal G-8
Niagara Falls H-7
North Bay G-7
Ottawa G-8
Prince Albert F-4
Prince George F-2
Prince Rupert E-1
Québec G-8
Regina G-4
Rivière-du-loup G-8
Saint John G-9
St. John's E-10
Saskatoon G-3
Sault Ste. Marie H-7
Sept-Iles F-8
Sherbrooke G-8
Sudbury G-7
Sydney F-10
Thompson F-4
Thunder Bay G-6
Toronto H-7
Trois-Rivières G-8
Vancouver G-1
Victoria G-1
Whitehorse D-1
Windsor H-7
Winnipeg G-5
Yellowknife D-3

MEXICO
(Map on page 72)
Pop.: 67,395,826
Area: 761,604 Sq. Mi.

Acapulco E-5
Chihuahua B-3
Ciudad Juárez A-3
Ciudad Obregon B-3
Ciudad Victoria C-5
Colima D-4
Culiacán C-3
Durango C-4
Fresnillo C-4
Guadalajara D-4
Hermosillo B-2
La Paz C-2
Matamoros C-6
Mérida D-8
Mexicali A-1
Mexico D-5
Monterrey C-5
Morelia D-5
Nuevo Laredo B-5
Oaxaca E-6
Piedras Negras B-5
Puebla D-5
Reynosa B-5
Saltillo C-5
San Luis Potosí C-5
Tampico C-5
Tijuana A-1
Toluca D-5
Torreón C-4
Veracruz D-6
Villahermosa E-7

Credits:
Managing Editor: Virginia O'Neill
Editor, writer: Barbara Ann Smutnik
Designer: Mary Jo Schrader
Original art: James Buckley
Cartographic Services: Michael Dobson
Production Services: Marianne Abraham